CW00686069

History of India

An Enthralling Overview of Significant Civilizations, Empires, Events, People, and Religion

Free limited time bonus

Stop for a moment. We have a free bonus set up for you. The problem is this: we forget 90% of everything that we read after 7 days. Crazy fact, right? Here's the solution: we've created a printable, 1-page pdf summary for this book that you're reading now. All you have to do to get your free pdf summary is to go to the following website:

https://livetolearn.lpages.co/enthrallinghistory/

Once you do, it will be intuitive. Enjoy, and thank you!

Table of Contents

Introduction

The history of India is the history of an entire subcontinent. Today's India is a third the size of the US or Europe, but its history includes parts of what are now Pakistan, Bangladesh, and even Afghanistan. It also had a huge influence on other Asian countries, both directly in Cambodia and Srivijaya (today's Indonesia) and indirectly through the export of Buddhism to Southeast Asia, China, and Tibet.

India contained some of the earliest civilizations of the world and has an immensely rich history. India seems to have absorbed new influences rather than replacing the old; so, today, it contains a little of everything: rich Hindu culture, memories of the Mughals in architecture and art, British bureaucracy (try booking a ticket on Indian Railways!), tribal art, and a thriving new IT industry. Now a democratic and officially secular nation, India retains its incredible diversity.

All that richness can make Indian history confusing. So can the fact that until recently, much Indian history was seen through colonial eyes. The British Raj saw Indian history as the story of dynasties and tried to separate and distinguish different races; it assumed that India never changed ("essentialism" or "orientalism"). Often, only Sanskrit texts were used to understand Indian history, and the Islamic contribution to India was overlooked, as were medieval Hindu movements.

And true to their "divide and rule" strategy, the Raj historians saw Indian history as a succession of mutually exclusive eras. They didn't really understand how, for instance, a single king in southern India might sponsor Jain, Buddhist, and Hindu faiths without partiality or how emperor Akbar blended his wife's Rajput, Hindu heritage with his dynasty's Turkic, Muslim roots.

Different ages overlap. India today contains First Peoples living in the Andaman Islands, tribal peoples such as the Gond and Munda, workers in call centers and IT companies, shoeshine men, and bicycle rickshaw drivers. You may meet a US tech company's CEO climbing a holy mountain barefoot or a traditional painter who quit her job in marketing to join the family art studio.

But the overlapping of different layers doesn't make India eternal. The early collection of religious poetry called the Vedic corpus, or Vedas, hasn't changed since a millennium before the Common Era, but the way the texts have been interpreted and used certainly has. This book will show you how religion developed over the ages and sometimes distinctly in different areas of India.

This book will help you navigate the different streams of Indian history without getting swamped. First, it takes a broadly chronological approach; then, at the end, there is the chance to look more at personalities, Indian culture, and India today.

Some earlier histories are based on the work of the 19th and early 20th centuries, which was affected by colonialism even where the individual historian had no ax to grind. This book uses work from writers like Shashi Tharoor, who has analyzed the "benefits" of the empire in a slightly different way, as well as William Dalrymple, who has used Persian-language texts to reinterpret Mughal history and the early days of the British in India.

It's a big ask to cram thousands of years of history into a small book. But if you want to learn about Indian history without having to read, for instance, the 24 different volumes of the *New Cambridge History of India*, hopefully this book will give you a good start.

Chapter 1: India: An Ancient Introduction

To get started in Indian history, you must first understand the huge dimensions of the task. India is big, and it has a very, very long history.

Consider, for instance, that India today has the world's second-largest population (next to China) and is the seventh-largest country by geographical area. The 2011 census gave India 1.2 billion residents, and this grew to nearly 1.4 billion in 2022. (The US, by comparison, has a total population of 331 million.)

India is not only a very large but also a very diverse country. Its 1.3 million square miles include the high Himalayas, several deserts, rainforests, coasts on two oceans, and at least six different climate zones. Lambada, in the north, is on roughly the same latitude as North Africa; Kanyakumari, on the southern tip, is on the same latitude as Ethiopia, the Gambia, or Ecuador. It goes from sea level to the top of Kanchenjunga at 8586 meters (28,170 feet)—the third-highest mountain in the world.

India is linguistically diverse, too, with twenty-two different officially recognized languages and many more unrecognized languages and dialects. About three-quarters of its languages come from the same Indo-Aryan family, with the unrelated Dravidian languages of South India (Tamil, Malayalam, Kannada, and Telegu) and two Sino-Tibetan languages (Manipuri and Bodo) making up most of the rest. Many Indians are multilingual, and educated Indians often speak Hindi,

English, and at least one other Indian language.

In terms of religion, India is 80 percent Hindu and about 14 percent Muslim, with substantial Christian, Sikh, and Jain minorities. It also has a Buddhist minority that increased when 100,000 Tibetan refugees headed to India after the Chinese took over Tibet (the Dalai Lama was one of them) and with the mass conversion of nearly half a million Untouchables led by B.R. Ambedkar.

Identities can be very fluid. Ladakhi grandmothers wearing traditional long dresses and aprons share work in the fields with their Ray-Ban-wearing grandsons doing an MBA at IIT Delhi. A priest in a temple, wearing his formal robes and a trident mark on his forehead, might turn out to be a former cricket player or marketing manager. India is a place where a Christian girl from a scheduled tribe can become a boxing champion and a member of the Rajya Sabha (equivalent to a senate), and a low-caste ragpicker (garbage collector) can become the mayor of a big city.

The geography of India partly dictated its history. Its location between Central Asia to the northwest and China to the northeast meant that India was always open to influence, invasion, or commerce, but the Himalayas also formed a significant barrier so that India always stood slightly apart. Passes from Central Asia include the Swat Valley, the Hunza Valley, and the Khyber Pass—the latter becoming extremely important as Britain and Russia competed in the "Great Game" to dominate the area in the nineteenth century. On the west coast, maritime trade with East Africa, the Middle East, and (later) Portugal and England created wealth, while from the east coast, Indian influence reached Thailand, Cambodia, Burma, and Indonesia.

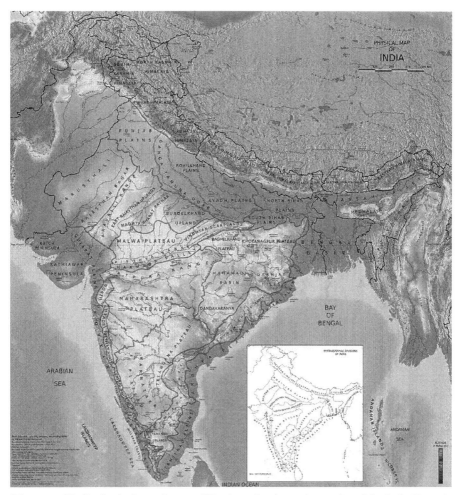

The map of India clearly shows the great Himalayan barrier to the north and the Indo-Gangetic Plain.

Within the subcontinent, regional differences are important, both geographically and culturally. India can be divided into three main regions: the north, from the Himalayas and the Hindu Kush down to the fertile Punjab (some of this area is now in Pakistan); the Gangetic plain of fertile silt, irrigated by the Ganges and Yamuna rivers; and the south, divided from the Gangetic plain by the Deccan Trap (an area of much-eroded volcanic basalt). Quite often, the history of each of these regions was different from that of others. For instance, while the Mughal Empire took over the north and the plains, it was never able to penetrate further south.

India's story began with a Paleolithic culture that used simple rock shelters. The most famous Stone Age site in India is Bhimbetka in central India, where over 750 rock shelters survive; cave paintings at Bhimbetka date from as early as 8,000 BCE. The earliest inhabitants of the site used basic stone tools such as flaked-off pebbles; later, in the Mesolithic period, they created new types of tools— microliths such as tiny arrowheads, which made hunting much easier. The paintings from this time depict themes of animals and hunting, as well as figures of pregnant women, showing a concern with fertility.

Mesolithic sites in other areas of northern and central India show that grain was being consumed since querns and rubbing stones for grinding flour have been found. Animal bones found at these sites include deer, boar, goat, and ostrich (the latter now extinct in India). Burials are often found inside the inhabited area, with grave goods; these people likely believed that the dead person's spirit would stay with them as part of the family, something that's found in other early cultures, such as Catal Huyuk in Turkey.

The Neolithic period saw a huge amount of progress. Agriculture became common, animals were domesticated, and pottery enabled better food storage; stone tools were now being highly polished, creating sharper edges and a striking improvement in efficiency. It's likely that small groups of Neolithic peoples overlapped across the country: remains have been found from this date in the Swat Valley and Kashmir and in the Godavari and Krishna valleys further south. Bhimbetka continued to be inhabited into historical times; later cave paintings show warriors on horseback or riding elephants.

While agriculture became advanced in the Chalcolithic period (2000-900 BCE), and the people of the ore-rich Aravalli Range developed metalworking in bronze and copper, these settlements don't appear to have developed into full-scale cities. It's likely the society of these settlements was relatively egalitarian, with a flat hierarchy and social structures based on clans. Many of these cultures would have still got a lot of their food from hunting or foraging, and agriculture may have been based at first on swidden cultivation—burning down an area of forest to use for a few years, then moving on once the soil was exhausted.

In later Indian texts, the forest becomes a scary place full of rakshasas (demons). For instance, in the Mahabharata, Krishna and Arjuna burn the Khandava forest totally to clear it for settlement. In the Ramayana, prince Rama is exiled from the city of Ayodhya to the forest with his wife and brother. Even now, you may be told not to go into the "jungle" (a wild place) "because there are bad people there."

It's difficult to tell when exactly this happened, but as agriculture became widespread and populations became more settled, a polarity emerged between the village and the wilderness (grama / aranya) and the field and the forest (kshetra / vana) that resounds in later Indian culture. One guess would be that this may have happened around the time the first cities were created, which is the theme of the next chapter.

Chapter 2: The Indus Valley Civilization and the Indo-Aryans

The Indus Valley Civilization began in the northwest of the subcontinent, where the Indus and numerous other rivers flow through a wide and fertile alluvial plain. The area where this civilization grew is now divided between India and Pakistan, and the two major sites, Harappa and Mohenjo-daro, are both in Pakistan; however, the culture spread as far south as Rajasthan and Gujarat and east towards the Ganges. Traces of the culture have even been found as far west as Oman in the Persian Gulf, showing that these Indians traded extensively.

The Indus Valley Civilization appears to have begun around the beginning of the third millennium BCE or slightly earlier and lasted until 1750 BCE. Many sites show continuous occupation during this time, with substantial continuity of culture between the pre-Harappan, mature, and late periods. However, this culture disappeared completely from sight after its decline; the major sites were only discovered and excavated in the 1920s and 1930s.

These cities are extensive in scale and mark the beginning of urban culture in India. Mohenjo-daro covers 200 hectares, and the lower town there may have had a population of 42,000. Even if pre-Harappan sites don't show huge technological advances, evidently the system of social organization needed to be significantly more complex than that of the rock-shelter culture.

	Date
Pre-Harappan	Late 4th millennium BCE or earlier
Early Harappan	3300-2600
Mature period of Indus civilization	2600-1900 BCE
Late period of Indus civilization	1900-1750 BCE

Trade networks became quite extensive, linking different communities and leading to a uniform material culture across the different sites that have been found. Numerous crops were cultivated, including peas and cotton, and the water buffalo was domesticated. By the end of the early period, seals already used the Harappan script, which has still not been deciphered. (This may have been a pictorial script or even a counting method. Most of the inscriptions that have been found are very short—the longest is only 34 characters long, and most include only five or six signs—which makes it particularly difficult to interpret.)

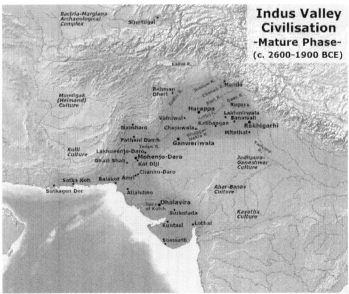

Map of the Indus Valley Civilization.

Indus Valley Civilization (IVC) cities had advanced town planning on a grid and a sanitation system, including the use of covered drains, as well as huge granaries allowing the inhabitants to store grain as insurance against drought. The massive walls of the cities may have been defensive but were also useful as protection against floods. Houses did not differ greatly in size or style, and almost all had access to wells for clean water; this gives the impression of a society without major extremes of wealth or poverty. Even in its ruined state, Mohenjo-daro is still very impressive.

Specialization of trades is already evident, with a concentration of particular trades in their own areas of the city. That's still the case in Indian towns today: all the candy makers are on one street, all the metalworkers on another.

The IVC had advanced metallurgy, including the use of lost-wax bronze casting and the use of copper, bronze, lead, tin, and various alloys, as well as gold. The IVC also developed a standardized system of weights and measures, and the use of a grid pattern for cities shows that the culture had some idea of surveying and geometry.

An intriguing feature of the IVC is that the cities appear not to have a sacred center. It seems likely, therefore, that religious ceremonies would have been carried out within the household. There are also no monumental tombs, as in other contemporary civilizations. One seal shows a seated figure with a horned headdress, surrounded by animals, which may be a sort of "horned god" figure, and female figurines may indicate a goddess cult, but archaeologists don't all agree with this interpretation.

The two greatest cities of the IVC, Harappa and Mohenjo-daro, flourished around 2600-2000 BCE. The cities then entered a decline and were eventually abandoned for reasons that remain unclear. It was earlier thought that an Aryan invasion destroyed the cities; however, it seems more likely that changes in the climate were responsible. The IVC had good drainage, but it did not have irrigation systems, which meant the cities were highly exposed to increases in temperature and changes in the course of rivers on which they depended. It seems likely that the people of the cities ended up making their way east towards the still-fertile Gangetic Plain.

Different cultures evolved elsewhere in India, but none were as spectacular as the Indus Valley culture. In the Indo-Gangetic Plain, iron was found by the first millennium BCE. Cut marks on bones show that cows were eaten; south of the Ganges, rice was cultivated, and terracotta animal figures are commonly found. There was a long continuity of small settlements, mainly of wattle and daub huts.

In the southern valleys of the Kaveri, Tungabhadra, Krishna, and Godavari rivers, small farming communities had emerged by the 3rd millennium BCE. They cultivated rice and millet and had sheep, goats, and buffalo. They buried their dead inside their huts—oddly, with their feet cut off.

By the first millennium, though, they had changed their burial rites and created megalithic sites for burial similar to those of non-Indian cultures. This was the time horses arrived in India, and harnesses are often found as grave goods together with hoes and sickles, as well as weapons. (Some later sites also include Roman coins, which shows how far Indian traders were voyaging.)

The Rig Veda and the Aryans

Around 1200 BCE is when India leaves prehistory and textual sources begin, including the Rig Veda and other Vedic texts. It is likely, though, that these texts were not written until considerably later but were transmitted orally for centuries. The main concern of these texts is to guide the reader in how to carry out religious rituals (a sort of instruction manual), so narrative is incidental and often has to be recreated from references that only hint at the myths.

In most areas, such as Europe or South and Central America, early cultures are known through their archeology but not through texts. In India, on the other hand, the early Aryan period is much better known through textual evidence, and there has been, until now, very limited archeological evidence.

Nineteenth and earlier 20th century historians believed that the Vedas were written by an Aryan people who had invaded from central Asia. However, the discovery of Harappan culture makes this theory unlikely. It seems more probable that there was a gradual migration of Aryan-language speakers and that existing Indian societies adapted (and adapted to) the newly arrived culture. It is intriguing that, though there is a linguistic link between the language of the Vedas and Old Iranian, gods and demons appear to have switched sides; the sun god Indra and the devas are "demons" in the Zend-Avesta (early Iranian scripture), while Ahura, a god in the Avesta, becomes the Indian Ashura, or demon.

Horse sacrifices are central in the Rig Veda as a means of proving the legitimacy of a ruler. Since no horses are known in the mid-Harappan, it seems likely that the new arrivals brought horses with them. On the other hand, it's quite notable that urban settlements, such as those at Mohenjo-daro and Harappa, are completely absent from the Rig Veda. It also doesn't mention exchange systems, so clearly the work was based on a very different form of society. (Rhinoceroses and tigers are shown on Harappan seals, but like towns, don't appear in the Rig Veda.)

Somewhat later than the Rig Veda, the two great epics Mahabharata (400 BCE) and Ramayana (500 BCE) were added, now written in pure Sanskrit. The Mahabharata tells the story of war set in the fertile plain around Delhi and likely recounts events that happened much earlier, perhaps around 950-800 BCE. In it, the Pandava brothers are set against the Kauravas, who have them exiled to the forest and later declare war on them. The Pandavas win with the help of Krishna, who gives one of them a philosophical lecture in the Bhagavad Gita (part of Book 6 of the Mahabharata). Krishna, a Yadava, is based in Dwarka, Gujarat, an area where the IVC still appears to have been active after the end of the Harappan cities.

As the action shifted from the Indus and Punjab to the Gangetic Plain, there was a gradual shift in the nature of agriculture and society. The Aryans were agro-pastoralists who used the cow as a measure of value and yokes of six or eight oxen to plow. They cultivated rice rather than wheat, which had been the staple of the north. They also came with new gods, the main deity being Agni, the god of fire, and worshiped them through sacrifices and other rituals. The hearth was the nucleus of worship in Aryan society. Other gods include the sun god Surya, Indra, Pushan, Savitri, and the death god Yama, as well as celestial beings like the Gandharvas.

(The word "Aryan" comes with a lot of baggage, having been used both by the British and later the Nazis to indicate a particular racial identity. We should really refer to them as "Aryan speakers." They appear to have been a linguistic community rather than a race and to have absorbed many of the existing communities in India over time.)

The Aryans appear to have brought with them the concept of a caste society, with four castes: the Brahmins or priests, the Kshatriya or rulers/warriors, the Vaishyas (farmers and merchants), and the Shudras (laborers). As mentioned, in the Veda, the concerns of the priests are primary; the reader is interested in how to perform rituals. However, by the time the Mahabharata was written, the Kshatriya clearly dominated; court politics, skirmishes, and fighting wars are its main subjects. The society that the Mahabharata describes is clearly very different from the flat society of the Indus Valley Civilization. The creation of the Shudra caste shows that labor has now become something that can be paid for, for instance.

In this regard, the practice of horse sacrifice is extremely important. A horse would have been an expensive investment, and the need for these costly sacrifices introduced a barrier to entry for clan chiefs and forced them to depend on the priests. This increased the status and power of the top two castes at the expense of the others.

Aryan religion is also based on the concepts of purity and pollution. Death, for instance, is a form of pollution; so is touching or eating and drinking with someone of an inferior caste. Aryan religion also introduced the idea of the cow as a sacred animal, with the result that cow dung and urine are considered pure in ritual terms. (Cow dung is actually used as a major source of fuel for both heating and cooking in traditional Indian life.)

This society must have looked a little like an early Celtic society, based on clans with chiefs who were involved in cattle raiding but also in extensive alliance-building through gift-giving. Genealogies started to become important at this time as temporary war leaders gave way to dynasties.

Re-emergence of Urban Culture

Around 600 BCE, towns began to re-emerge, mainly in the Ganges Basin, and tended to be located in the hills flanking the basin rather than on the plain itself. Commercial centers arose at Champa, Rajagriha, Kaushambi, Kashi (Varanasi), Vaishali, Shravasti, Ujjain, and Taxila. Around 500 BCE, Kaushambi appears to have had a population of around 36,000—a significantly-sized city. Wet rice cultivation in this area could yield three crops a year, creating a significant agricultural surplus that could support the population of the cities.

Towns such as Kaushambi, Rajagriha, and Shravasti covered large areas. They traded long-distance, particularly for luxury items, and coinage was introduced around this time. It is possible that the first coinage was the invention of market professionals, rather than rulers, aimed at meeting their needs for a more secure and simpler method of exchange than barter.

The change in social organization from a chieftain-led raiding culture to an urban culture of gana-sanghas (assemblies) created a new intellectual environment. Debate between competing ideologies and philosophies became common. At the same time, the number of castes went from four to two: Kshatriya, the ruling class, and dasa-karmakara, laborers and/or slaves. The language also changed from Sanskrit to Prakrit, which became the lingua franca of a large area of India.

New Hindu sects were started around this time, including the monastic Ajivikas and the materialist Charvakas. It was in this environment that two great religious leaders were born: Mahavira, founder of the Jain religion at Vaishali, and Shakyamuni Buddha in Kapilavastu. In many ways, their teachings were similar, including a stress on ahimsa, nonviolence. Some Jain ascetics even wear masks so they don't inadvertently breathe in gnats and other small creatures.

Both Buddha and Mahavira saw the goal of life as purification or enlightenment. Both created monastic communities of ascetics, perhaps drawing on urban culture for the idea of a custom-made community. Certainly, it would have been difficult to establish such monasteries without the existence of wealthy towns that could supply them with donations.

Buddha was born a prince of the Shakya clan, but having seen old age, sickness, and death, was shaken out of his comfortable lifestyle and spent years searching for truth until he finally achieved enlightenment. He evolved the doctrine of the Four Noble Truths: (1) all beings experience suffering, (2) suffering arises from desire and attachment, (3) liberation from attachment brings liberation from suffering, and (3) the eightfold path (symbolized by the eight-spoked wheel) can bring any human being to enlightenment.

Buddhism appears to have been initially a non-deistic philosophy. It also supported social freedom, refusing to recognize caste, and replaced the idea of divine kings with the theory of a social contract. Both Buddhists and Jains, in fact, made the two top castes useless: priests were not needed since sacrificial rites were not required, and warriors would have to rethink their status to suit the new ethic of nonviolence.

The Maurya Empire

The next major change in Indian history came in the fourth century BCE with the creation of the Maurya Empire. Chandragupta Maurya, the first emperor, took over the Magadha state, which had expanded to cover most of the Ganges Basin. He then expanded his lands towards the Indus in the north, where Alexander the Great had left a power vacuum behind after an inconclusive invasion. He took Persian territories in Afghanistan and Baluchistan, including Gandhara, where a Buddhist style of art that reflected the Hellenistic art of the time had evolved.

But Chandragupta doesn't appear to have been a diehard warrior. At the end of his career, he abdicated in favor of his son Bindusara and became a Jain ascetic.

Bindusara continued the expansion of his campaigns in the Deccan, but his son Ashoka brought the Mauryan Empire to its height. Ashoka is referred to as Chakravartin (world ruler) in Buddhist texts. He transformed the infrastructure of India, for instance building the Great North Road from Taxila (now in Pakistan) to Pataliputra (now Patna). This route was the Great Trunk Road of the British Raj and then National Highway No. 1 until 2010; it has now been renumbered No. 3 and No. 44, running all the way from the Pakistan border to New Delhi.

Ashoka took the task of standardizing the law seriously and made inscriptions of his edicts in Brahmi script across his empire. (He also used Greek and Aramaic languages in some places since these languages were spoken across the Persian Empire and there were still many Greek communities in Ashoka's domains.) In the Ganges Plain, he used rock pillars; elsewhere, texts were inscribed directly onto rock faces. These edicts present the earliest writing that survives in India apart from the still-undeciphered Harappan script.

Shocked by the violence of his campaign against Kalinga in eastern India, Ashoka converted to Buddhism a few years later. Unlike many rulers of his time, he refers to his personal experiences in some of his inscriptions: "Directly, after the Kalingas had been annexed, began His Sacred Majesty's zealous protection of the Law of Piety, his love of that Law, and his inculcation of that Law. Thence arises the remorse of His Sacred Majesty for having conquered the Kalingas because the conquest of a country previously unconquered involves the slaughter, death, and carrying away captive of the people. That is a matter of profound sorrow and regret to His Sacred Majesty" (Smith, 185). Perhaps he inherited this element of his nature from his grandfather, though he adopted the Buddhist religion rather than Jain asceticism.

Ashoka's edicts endorse nonviolence, doing good deeds, and generosity. In some of the minor edicts, he refers to his conversion, although he supported other religious bodies, such as the Ajivikas and—like other emperors after him—aimed to create a pluralistic state in which all faiths were respected.

The Ashoka pillar at Vaishala.
Amaan Imam, CC BY-SA 4.0 <https://creativecommons.org/licenses/by-sa/4.0>, via Wikimedia Commons; https://commons.wikimedia.org/wiki/File:N-BR-39_Ashokan_Pillar_Vaishali_%282%29.jpg

Ashoka's capital at Pataliputra (Patna) was strategically positioned between northern India and the Indo-Gangetic Plain. To the south, he had friendly relations with the Cholas, Pandyas, and Keralaputras (Cheras). He had close links with Lanka, where his son Mahinda is said to have been a Buddhist missionary, and gifted it with a branch of the Bodhi Tree under which Buddha received enlightenment.

The Maurya Empire was a largely agrarian empire where the state controlled the irrigation system and used tax revenues to pay for it. Archeology shows that the empire had a high standard of living, with brick houses, stone palaces in Pataliputra, and highly polished stone sculptures. Ashoka planted trees along the roads for shelter from the sun and built watering places along the major routes. He created provincial administrations at Ujjain, Taxila, and Suvarnagiri (Kanakagiri) and maybe also at Girnar and Dhauli; around the periphery of his empire, though, people were still living in megalithic societies.

Ashoka created what has been seen as a golden age for India. However, his successors failed to keep his empire in good health. The ninth and last Mauryan ruler was replaced in a military coup by his general, Pushpamitra, founder of the Shunga dynasty, around 185 BCE. The Shunga continued to rule Magadha in the east of the Ganges Basin, while northern areas such as Punjab, Haryana, and Rajasthan returned to clan-based rule.

The absence of strong rulership in northern India allowed the Central Asian empire of the Kushans to occupy the country as far south as Sarnath and Varanasi. The Kushans established trade along the Silk Roads between China and what is now Uzbekistan and as far as Rome in the west. It was these new trade routes that helped spread Buddhism to China; later, the Chinese would export Buddhism to Japan and other Asian nations.

South India saw the beginnings of state formation later than the north. Towns such as Madurai, Uraiyur, and Karur became established, and dynasties such as the Chola established their rule over large areas around the third century BCE. Around the same time, the Sangam literary corpus was established. Written in Tamil, it is very different from northern literature. The majority of it focuses on romantic and erotic subjects, with only a small amount of epic verse.

Buddhism and Jainism had become highly influential by the second century BCE, when the Great Stupa at Sanchi was built, together with numerous monasteries; another stupa was erected at Bharhut. At first, a majority of donations for the structures came from small landowners, artisans, and guilds, as well as from monks and nuns. (Note that relics, which stupas were built to enclose, are incompatible with Brahman rules of purity.)

The Vedic religion did not have sacred buildings; it was based on sacrifice, and sacrificial sites were temporary. Thus, it appears to have been the two newer religions that introduced the concept of sacred architecture in India. Rock-cut chaitya halls and viharas (monasteries) imitated wooden designs to begin with (for instance, at Karla, an early site) and are often relatively small in scale. But they soon increased in both size and complexity. Sites such as Ellora and Ajanta represent a further development; at Ellora, Hindu, Jain, and Buddhist works are all found at the same site and was often paid for by the same patrons.

Buddhism was originally aniconic; Buddha was not shown as a figure but represented by signs of his status, such as a parasol, an empty seat, or a miniature stupa. For instance, there is a bell-shaped stupa with a wooden parasol above it at the end of the Karla chaitya hall whereas, in a modern Buddhist temple, a statue of the Buddha would be expected. As time passed, Buddha started to be represented in human form, and influences from Hinduism later introduced other beings, such as protective gods, bodhisattvas, and so on.

The Gupta Empire

The next great empire in India was that of the Guptas, founded by Chandragupta I (not to be confused with Chandragupta Maurya) in 319 CE. The Gupta Empire has often been regarded as a golden age. Unlike the Maurya Empire, it was not highly centralized but allowed most decisions to be made locally.

Chandragupta married a Lichchhavi princess of Vaishali and extended his rule as far west as Allahabad and as far north as Nepal. However, the empire did not extend much farther south than the Ganges. His son, Samudragupta, expanded the empire much further into the Deccan, as far south as Tamil Nadu, north to Rajasthan and Punjab, and east into Bengal. However, it seems likely that many of these territories simply paid him tribute and managed their own affairs. In other words, he had financial but not political control. This appears to have been an effective formula, as the Gupta Empire would last until 532 CE—more than two centuries.

The Guptas made land grants an important feature of their rule, restructuring agriculture by giving grants to encourage the conversion of wasteland. Such grants were given to individuals, as well as to monasteries, temples, and seats of learning, such as the Buddhist university of Nalanda, which at one point owned 200 villages. (Xuanzang, a Chinese monk who visited India from 629-645, studied at Nalanda and describes it as an earthly paradise, with pools filled with blue lotus flowers, dazzling flame-tree flowers, and groves of mango trees for shade. When he returned to China, he took numerous Sanskrit texts with him, making a huge contribution to the expansion of Buddhism in China. Much later, in the sixteenth century, novelist Wu Cheng'en adapted his experiences as Journey to the West, or Monkey. You may have seen the TV series or played the videogame.)

Land grants were inscribed on copper plates, a good number of which survived. Clearly, there was now a bureaucracy and complex legal structure in which written records were important. An intriguing feature of the land grant system is that it allowed small-scale peasant agriculture to coexist with large-scale land ownership and infrastructure projects, such as dams and stepwells (wells with staircases built for easy access to groundwater level).

Hinduism, perhaps at least partly motivated by the challenge from the two "reform" religions, had moved on from Vedic times. Agni and Surya, the most important gods of the earlier period, faded; Vishnu and Shiva replaced them as the major gods, with shakti, or goddess cults, also emerging. Unlike the Vedic religion, which appears to have had no images of the gods, Hinduism now represented the god by an idol, lingam (phallic symbol), or rock. Animal sacrifices were now being replaced by puja, which involved giving grain or other vegetables to the deity, and darshan, viewing the sacred image, which is often hidden behind a gate or curtain that is opened to allow the worshiper to see the god.

However, the word "Hinduism" at this date is something of a misnomer since worshipers would have identified themselves as Vaishnava (worshiping Vishnu), Shaiva (worshiping Shiva), or Pashupata (another form of Shiva worship). The label "Hindu" arrived much later—in fact, with the Islamic invasions.

Nonetheless, the cults of different gods appear to have coexisted without problems, perhaps because they shared common philosophies and a common social structure.

Chapter 3: Medieval India and Its Empires (600-1450 CE)

Over nearly ten centuries, many civilizations and kingdoms came and went in India, and India also exported its culture elsewhere. For instance, the Mon kingdom (predecessor of Thailand) became Buddhist, though many Hindu rites were also built into the Thai form of Buddhism. Hindu rites such as the Royal Plowing Ceremony are particularly important to the Thai royal family, perhaps reflecting the way the horse sacrifice was used to legitimize Aryan kings. The Khmer Empire of the ninth to fifteenth centuries and the Srivijaya (Indonesian) empire of the seventh to twelfth centuries also incorporated both Hinduism and Buddhism.

China and Tibet also became Buddhist, and Chinese Buddhism reached Korea and then Japan just before 600 CE. However, China did not integrate Indian culture in the same way as the Southeast Asian countries, likely because it already had a highly developed imperial culture.

By this date, India was a highly sophisticated society that had already seen two major empires and had advanced scientific knowledge. For instance, before 499, the mathematician Aryabhata had calculated pi to four decimal places and understood how the earth rotated on its axis and how lunar eclipses occurred. Arab scholars, who had access to both ancient Greek and Indian mathematics, thought the Indians were more interesting and accomplished than the Greeks.

Southern India in the Middle Ages

A significant change during the medieval period was the emergence of the south and the Deccan compared to the dominance of northern India and the Indo-Gangetic Plain in earlier periods. Though dynasties came and went, in most cases, the rulers of different areas appear to have been evenly matched. So, despite tensions and occasional wars, no conclusive victory created a new empire with anything like the reach of the Maurya or Gupta empires.

In Tamil Nadu, there were two main dynasties: the Pandyas in Madurai ruling the south and the Palas, or Pallavas, in Kanchipuram ruling the north. The second Pallava emperor, Mahendravarman I (ruled c. 600-630), was a musician, poet, painter, and scholar; he was also responsible for creating the earliest temples in Mamallapuram, which were cut out of rock. Unlike earlier rock-cut architecture, though, the rock was cut down on each side to leave the temples freestanding.

During Mahendravarman's rule, wars with the Chalukya dynasty, which ruled in Badami, Karnataka, began; they continued under his son, Narasimhavarman. The balance swung back and forth, with each side reaching the other's capital at one point but unable to hold it.

A rock-cut temple at Mamallapuram with a rock-cut elephant.

The Chalukyas were ruling at Badami by 543 when Pulakeshin I made a cliff inscription; he used both Sanskrit and the Kannada language. The Chalukyas continued to rule the Deccan Plateau for over 600 years, though their fortunes waxed and waned over the years. They were particularly important in developing the southern style of temple architecture, building temples at Badami, Aihole, and Pattadakal. The earliest temples at Badami were rock-cut, but later temples had finely made perforated screens on the windows, spires over the central shrine, and a pillared mandapa hall in front of the sanctuary.

Meanwhile, the southwestern kingdom of Kerala was ruled by the Chera Perumal dynasty. Kerala always seems to have remained slightly apart from the other kingdoms, though that never stopped the Pandyas from attempting to slice off parts of central Kerala for themselves.

The Rashtrakuta were a small clan that served the Chalukyas for many years. But in 753, Dantidurga Rashtrakuta turned against the Chalukyas and defeated them. He allied his new kingdom with the Pallavas, helping Nandivarman II regain his capital Kanchipuram from the Chalukyas, who had taken it. Nandivarman then married Dantidurga's daughter, linking the two dynasties. At their height around 850 to 900, the Rashtrakutas ruled most of India south of the Ganges and controlled the western seaboard and trade with Arabia. Dantidurga's successor Krishna I built the immense rock-cut Kailash temple at Ellora; this was an immensely wealthy and ambitious house.

However, the Rashtrakutas didn't have the staying power of the Chalukyas. From 972 onward, Rashtrakuta power declined, and by the end of the century, the Chalukyas had made a comeback. (The last Rashtrakuta emperor, Indra IV, became a Jain ascetic and took the vow of Sallekhana, gradually starving himself to death.)

These southern states mixed a number of different types of land tenure. Villages might pay tax on the land that they cultivated; some villages were donated to an individual or group or to a temple. Temple villages became more important as time went on. They also typically mixed different religions, though Buddhism gradually began to weaken, and royal patronage shifted towards Hindu and Jain foundations. At Badami, there are both Jain and Hindu rock-cut temples, and even though the Pallavas were Hindu, they sponsored a number of Jain temples, for example in Kanchipuram and Chitharal.

This period also saw the creation of the matha or mutt, a Hindu version of the Buddhist or Jain monastic community.

A large number of hero stones from the south have survived, most of them dating from 300 to about 1200. They commemorate the death of a hero in battle and are generally divided into a number of panels showing battle scenes, the hero worshiping a deity, and the hero in a palanquin or riding his horse. These stones may have served as the focus of a local cult.

Around 907, the Cholas, whose state was based around the Kaveri River, vastly increased their power. By the time of Rajaraja I (reigned 985-1014), the Cholas controlled most of Tamil Nadu, Kerala, and part of Karnataka, as well as northern Sri Lanka. Rajaraja built Thanjavur/Tanjore's "Big Temple" (the Brihadisvara or Rajarajesvarem Temple), which is considered one of the greatest of all the temples built in the southern style, with its 217-foot-high vimana tower. The Cholas supported Shaivism, giving their patronage to the temple of the dancing Shiva (Shiva Nataraja) at Chidambaram. By the late twelfth century, though, both the Cholas and the Chalukyas started to weaken, and things seem to have fallen apart quickly.

In the final centuries of the medieval period in India, two new dynasties, the Hoysala and Kakatiya, rose on the west coast in Karnataka. By 1245, the Hoysalas had taken over the Chola kingdom and most of the Pandyas' lands in southern Tamil Nadu. The Hoysalas, unlike the Shaivite Cholas, were a Vaishnavite house influenced by Sri Ramanuja (1077-1157), who stressed bhakti (devotion) as a means to salvation.

In the Deccan, too, this was a time of change; the Yadavas, or Seuna, based in Devagiri (now Daulatabad), expanded as far north as Gujarat.

During the entire medieval period, towns continued to increase in importance. For instance, the Jain pilgrimage center Shravanabelagola developed from a pure shrine into a major merchant town. The establishment of trading associations and local craft guilds show that commercial success now forced artisans and merchants to create new institutions to manage their businesses; however, they do not seem to have aspired to political power.

At the same time, there was a striking increase in temple building. Tanjore's temple received donations from as far away as Sri Lanka, while Rajendra Chola (Rajaraja's son) founded a massive temple at Gongaikondacholapuram, a mouthful that means "The City to which the

Cholas brought the Ganges" since he had conquered Odisha and Bengal and had pots of Ganges water sent back to his capital. (Rajendra also conquered Srivijaya and part of Burma, a rare act of foreign expansionism; most Indian kings restricted their ambitions to the subcontinent.)

Rock-cut temples gave way to freestanding temple buildings by the end of the period, often with multiple concentric courtyards surrounding the temple (as at Srirangam, where the temple occupies 155 acres with seven concentric enclosures). The main temple spire often reached impressive heights, but it was now also surrounded by gopuras, or gateway towers, often at all four cardinal directions. Large halls were added for recitations of devotional poetry. Temple communities developed to a huge size; Tanjore's main temple had 600 employees, including dancers, cooks, and musicians, as well as priests.

A gopura at the Sri Ranganathasamy Temple Rajagopuram, Srirangam, Tiruchirapalli
Writer hit, CC BY-SA 4.0 <https://creativecommons.org/licenses/by-sa/4.0>, via Wikimedia Commons; https://commons.wikimedia.org/wiki/File:Srirangam_Temple_Gopuram_View.jpg

The Tamil poets, known as the Alvars (Vaishnavite) and Nayanars (Shaivite), flourished in the early Middle Ages, writing devotional poetry that influenced the bhakti movement. Their work often draws a parallel between kings and gods; the temple is shown as the palace of the deity, and the idol is given a lifestyle like a king's.

Northern India in the Middle Ages

Meanwhile, in northern India, three great empires overlapped: the Rashtrakuta in the Deccan, the Gurjara-Pratiharas in Malwa (today's Madhya Pradesh) and Gujarat, and the Pala or Dharma kings in Bengal and Bihar. Kannauj, the city where the three realms met, was the focal point of the conflict between them, which is often referred to as the Tripartite Struggle.

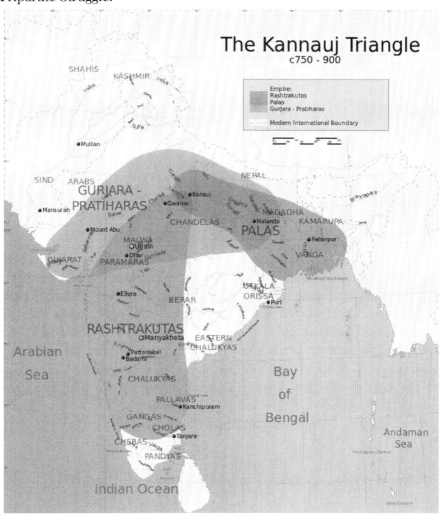

The Tripartite Struggle between three kingdoms. Note how Kannauj is right in the middle of the disputed area.

w:user:Planemad, CC BY-SA 3.0 <https://creativecommons.org/licenses/by-sa/3.0>, via Wikimedia Commons; https://commons.wikimedia.org/wiki/File:Indian_Kanauj_triangle_map.svg

The Pala dynasty greatly increased the agricultural exploitation of the eastern Indo-Gangetic Plain with widespread rice cultivation. They also had commercial interests in Southeast Asia, and their wealth enabled them to give significant patronage to Buddhist institutions such as the university at Nalanda. However, their attempts to push south were repelled by the Chola; this seems to have set quite a firm line between north and south.

In the northwest, Rajput clans became dominant, many of them claiming descent from the sun god Surya (as the Maharanas of Mewar, in Udaipur, still do) or from Rama. Others said they were descended from a sacrificial fire on Mount Abu. The rulers may not originally have been from the Kshatriya caste, but their newly-created genealogies, together with the acquiescence of the Brahmin priests, enabled them to step up to their new caste and legitimize their rule.

This northern society appears to have been less developed than in the south. For instance, hero stones marking the memory of heroes killed in battle or in cattle raids are found two centuries later in the Rajput territories than in southern India. Land ownership was also considerably less developed in terms of types of tenure.

Northern temple architecture developed in a different style than in the south. The basics of the temple are similar: there is a cave-like shrine with a shikhara spire over it, preceded by one or more vestibules, often with a walkway around the sanctuary. Unlike southern straight-sided towers, the shikhara is usually curved. The biggest difference from the southern style is that the whole temple is usually raised on a high plinth, giving it a much more impressive profile. Towards the end of the Middle Ages, highly ornate carving became usual. Perhaps the best example is the Dilwara Jain Temple complex on Mount Abu, which has minutely detailed, delicate carvings in fine white marble.

In Orissa, the temples of Bhubaneshwar, the Jagannath Temple in Puri, and the Sun Temple of Konarak all date from this period. In Bundelkhand, the Chandela dynasty built the Khajuraho temples, including both Jain and Hindu sanctuaries, which are notorious for their erotic imagery.

The Jagannath Temple in Puri by night. Note the pyramidal mandapa roofs and the curved sides of the shikhara spire.

Kalyanpuranand, CC BY-SA 4.0 <https://creativecommons.org/licenses/by-sa/4.0>, via Wikimedia Commons; https://commons.wikimedia.org/wiki/File:Lord_Jagannath_temple_at_night.jpg

However, while the balance of power teetered between these various Indian dynasties, a new threat was massing on the northern frontier. India was used to trading with the Arabs and saw them as a source of revenue, but the Turkic Muslims of Central Asia were a different kettle of fish—they were intent on raiding, not trading. Mahmud of Ghazni led seventeen separate raids down from the barren Hindu Kush into India; in 1018, he destroyed Mathura, taking away huge amounts of gold and silver. In 1023, it was Gwalior's turn, which decided to pay him protection money rather than risk seeing its city sacked. In 1025, Mahmud raided Gujarat and destroyed the Somnath Temple, taking its great doors. (Lord Ellenborough, believing that Mahmud had reused these doors in his mausoleum in Afghanistan, had them ripped off during the Battle of Kabul in 1842 and brought back to India. However, they are clearly northern since they're made of deodar wood, and deodars don't grow in Gujarat. They're also clearly ornamented in an Islamic style, with geometrical figures such as six-pointed stars. They are now kept in a side room at Agra Fort.)

Muhammad Ghuri, who invaded at the end of the twelfth century, took things a step further than simply raiding. Rather than going home with the loot, he intended from the first to create his own kingdom in India. In 1182, he conquered Sind and then started looking farther south. While at the First Battle of Tarain in 1191, he was unsuccessful; after the Second Battle of Tarain in 1192, he was able to take control of Delhi. Ghori was assassinated in 1206, so he didn't get to enjoy his new sultanate all that long, but the damage had been done. The Delhi Sultanate now became the nucleus of a new political entity and of the Muslim religion in India; it also became a staging post for further expeditions south as far as Karnataka, where five separate Bahmani sultanates emerged.

In the south, the Vijayanagar Empire had become prominent in the late Middle Ages, leaving the immense ruins of its capital Vijayanagara at Hampi. For a long time, Vijayanagar held out, sometimes playing one sultanate against another, but eventually, the five Bahmani sultanates banded together against the empire; they destroyed it in the Battle of Talikota in 1565. (Today, it's one of the chief backpacker centers in India, with its ruins spread out over several square miles along the Tungabhadra River.)

Culturally, the highlight of this era was the bhakti movement. Rather than stressing ritual, it stressed the direct relationship between the bhakta (devotee) and their god. Many bhakti devotional poems are written as love poems. Women and lower castes were liberated from the constraints of Brahmanical demands for "purity" and took an active role in the movement.

Sri Ramanuja (1077-1157) gave this tradition a philosophical underpinning. For him, salvation (moksha) couldn't be achieved simply through knowledge but must come through bhakti yoga, the discipline of devotion. He saw moksha not simply as freedom from further rebirths but as a state of joy in which the soul can continuously contemplate and enjoy divine perfection. He also fought for the lower castes to be admitted to temples and for non-Brahmins to be involved in the practice of puja.

Jayadeva's Gita Govinda, written in the twelfth century, is a set of poems telling the story of Radha's love for Krishna. Their separations and eventual reconciliation are symbolic of the soul's distraction from the love of god and its eventual return through devotion; in many ways, Radha becomes a symbol of and role model for the bhakta. Each poem has its raga or musical mode noted, and Jayadeva is said to have sung one of the compositions each night in the temple of Jagannath at Puri, a tradition that continues today.

Chaitanya Mahaprabhu (1486-1534) was born in Bengal and became an ecstatic devotee of Krishna; some people even regarded him as an avatar of Krishna. It is Chaitanya who was responsible for rediscovering the sacred forests around Vrindavan, where Krishna spent his life with Radha and the gopis (cow-girls); he also popularized the chanting of Hare Krishna.

Even Muslims could follow the path of bhakti. Kabir, born in 1398, was the son of a Muslim weaver, but his poetry dismisses both Muslim and Hindu rites and dogma and advocates looking into the devotee's own heart to find the presence of god. Both Hindus and Muslims disowned him while he was alive and claimed him after his death; the Sikhs later included some of his poetry in their scripture, the Adi Granth.

In some ways, Guru Nanak, the founder of Sikhism, can be seen as coming from a bhakti tradition. He was born in 1469 in Punjab to a merchant family and developed a spirituality based on the equality of all believers, good actions, and fraternity. He traveled extensively, visiting major pilgrimage centers of both Hindu and Muslim faiths, and emphasized bhakti as a way of integrating spiritual practice into practical daily life.

Originally, Sikhism was a peaceful religion, but persecution of the Sikhs from the time of emperor Jahangir turned the Sikhs into a militant sect. (This will be covered in the next chapter). The Guru Granth Sahib, the scripture of the Sikhs, is a pluralistic work; it's written in Gurmukhi script but includes Persian, Braj Bhasha, Prakrit, and Sanskrit texts, as well as Punjabi; it also includes verses by Kabir and the Hindu bhakti poet Ravidas, as well as teaching from the Islamic mystic, Baba Farid.

Chapter 4: The Mughal Empire: A Struggle for Supremacy

The Mughal Empire is perhaps one of the world's most well-known early modern empires, but its roots were in failure. The failure was Babur, prince of Fergana and great-great-great-grandson of Timur, or Tamerlane as he was known to the West.

Timur was a spectacularly successful man. He was a Turkic nomad who managed to conquer the Chagatai Khanate, which descended from Genghis Khan. He then led military campaigns across Central Asia, becoming the leading ruler of the Islamic world and making his capital in Samarkand. Timur actually invaded India and sacked Delhi in 1398. Understanding that elephants were easily panicked, he put his enemy's forces to rout by sending fire camels against them—that is, camels with hay piled high on their backs and then set on fire. However, other things soon distracted Timur from pursuing his Indian excursion.

Babur took after Timur in being valiant and smart but was, unfortunately, a serial failure. He won Samarkand but then he lost Fergana; he then managed to lose Samarkand three separate times. Clearly, Timur's inheritance was not going to fall into his hands. In the end, he decided to turn east and then south, taking Kabul, where he set up his rule, and then heading into India. And there, finally, his luck began to change.

Babur is a fascinating figure. He left an autobiography, the Baburnama, which is a strange mix of diplomacy, warfare, and natural history. On one page, he describes how his men built a tower of severed enemy heads after a battle; on the next, he discusses where to find the best muskmelons or describes different varieties of parrots. In between, he did a lot of partying: the founder of the Mughal Empire was, in fact, a drug fiend.

It took him five separate expeditions to figure out that India was not just a source of wealth and bananas but a good place to create a new empire. The Delhi sultanate had always been weakened by dissension and dynastic squabbles, making it a clear target, so that was where he focused. In the Battle of Panipat of 1526, Babur defeated Ibrahim Lodi of Delhi, and the Delhi sultanate became the beginning of the Mughal Empire.

However, Delhi was a small place, and it was surrounded by enemies, including the Rajputs in the north, who could easily cut it off from Kabul. The Rajputs were a much stronger enemy than the Delhi sultanate. Rana Sanga of Mewar (Udaipur) succeeded in getting the different Rajput clans to unite against the invader, creating a 200,000-strong army. (Numbers at this period are always approximate and often exaggerated, and it's Babur who gives this number, so take it with a grain of salt.)

At the Battle of Khanwa (1527), Babur, a fine strategist, built a fortified position and raked the Rajputs with artillery and musket fire without engaging in close combat. This allowed him to draw the sting of the Rajput charge. He also kept his horsemen back, ready for a flanking move. Only when the Rajputs attacked the Mughal flanks did Babur loose his army on them; Rana Sanga was shot and concussed, and Babur took advantage of the resulting confusion to take the offensive and completely rout the Rajput forces.

Panipat is often considered one of the most important battles ever fought in India. Arguably, though, Khanwa was even more important. It brought Hindu rulers under Babur's empire, and Babur, being a smart ruler, accepted Hindus into both his army and his administration. The Mughal Empire became a mixed empire where all faiths were tolerated and a major trading center, exporting prettily painted and embroidered cloth to Europe. (The French called these "indiennes," while the English called them by their Hindi name, "chintz.")

Babur's version of Islam was liberal. He used drugs and drank alcohol, and like the Persians of his day, he saw nothing wrong in figurative art or music. The Taliban would definitely not have approved.

He did, however, impose the jizya tax on non-Muslims in his empire.

Babur died in 1530 at just 47, having turned his initial failure into brilliant success. His son Humayun, unfortunately, was not able to keep things together. First, he was challenged for the throne by his brothers Kamran, Askari, and Hindal. Then he was pushed out of India again by Sher Shah Suri, a warlord who had created his own state in Bengal. He spent many years in Persia, where Shah Tahmasp gave him refuge.

But in 1555, Humayun was able to reclaim his throne, as well as his son Akbar, who had been left behind in Kabul when Humayun fled. He lasted less than a year, slipping on the steps of his library and dying of his injuries three days later.

Akbar succeeded to the throne at just thirteen years old. He was an unruly, self-willed, obstinate, and functionally illiterate boy, but he also had vast physical courage and daring and intense curiosity. He rode male elephants in musth (an aggressive, testosterone-fueled mood), swam rivers swollen with monsoon rains, and occasionally went berserk with rage. But he was also intelligent and learned quickly. By relying on speed and firepower and introducing innovations such as camel and elephant-mounted swiveling guns, he changed the rules of war and made his forces virtually impossible to defeat. He even invented rockets with shrieking whistles tied to them, which would drive his enemies' horses mad with their wailing sound.

Akbar with a lion and a lamb, from an album belonging to Shah Jahan. It clearly shows the eclectic nature of the Mughal court, with little angels in the sky and a crown clearly copied from European originals.

Akbar wasn't just a military genius; he was also a smart ruler like his grandfather. For instance, he realized that as long as the empire relied only on central Asian nobles (the Turani), it would not be easy to govern and would not have support from the people. To end the Turanis' dominance, he brought in Persian and Rajput administrators and created the mansab system in which land grants (jagirs) were related to the rank of the holder and were regularly rotated rather than hereditary. He also started minting square rupees, creating a coinage that could soon be used across his entire empire and abolishing the jizya tax on Hindus.

Though initially ruling only in name, Akbar soon took over for his regent and expanded his empire. In 1567, he took the fortress of Chittor, formerly considered impregnable; he had already taken Mandu, Malwa, and Gondwana. After this, several other Rajput rajas decided to join the Mughals voluntarily, bringing Bikaner, Bundelkhand, and Jaisalmer under his control. At Chittor, the women of the fort committed jauhar, immolating themselves in a fire while the men dressed in holy saffron garments and issued out of the fort on what was clearly a suicide mission. (This may well have shocked Akbar as much as it shocks us; he passed a law against women being forced to commit sati, though allowing voluntary sati.)

Akbar also married a Rajput woman, Harkha Bai, known in the Mughal court as Mariam-uz-Zamani, who was the mother of the next emperor, Jahangir. Other Rajput wives followed, bringing their own religion and customs to the Mughal court. Thus, instead of being an Islamic conqueror, Akbar became the head of a mixed-race, mixed-religion, syncretic court.

At his new capital of Fatehpur Sikri, Akbar created a new kind of architecture, again mixing influences from Islamic Central Asia with native Indian styles. His buildings have Indian chhatri pavilions but also huge arches, which come from Iranian mosque styles. In the Diwan-i-Khas, his private audience hall, four stone walkways in the air connected stairs at the corners of the building to a central column supporting Akbar's throne, a stunning and unique conception of the emperor seated in the air. (The palace also included a small temple where his Hindu wife could worship.) There are also domes, which were unknown in India before the Mughals but became a regular motif of Mughal architecture.

Akbar may also have invented his own religion, though this depends on how you interpret his desire for sulh-i-kul, "universal harmony." Some historians have suggested that he set up a syncretist religion in which he served as a deputy for god. It's perhaps more likely that he had a small clique with special admissions rituals within which he and members of his court conducted their spiritual investigations—a religious club, so to speak, rather than a cult. What's certain is that in addition to taking Hindus into his court, Akbar welcomed at least three Jesuit missionaries, as well as Jewish scholars, to his debates. His curiosity was intense, and this included religion, as well as warfare and architecture.

This was a golden age of the arts. The environment in Persia was becoming increasingly intolerant, which allowed Akbar to recruit many Persian artists and artisans; he also brought the famed musician Tansen from Gwalior and hired Indian painters. Though he was illiterate, Akbar loved to be read to, and he sponsored the translation of works like the Mahabharata from the Indian languages into Persian.

Akbar was not the first Mughal emperor, but he was the first wholly Indian Mughal emperor. Under him, India became the center of the world economically, greater than any other empire of the time. And it continued to increase in size. In 1575, he took Bihar and Bengal from the Afghan chief Daud Khan, and the next year he defeated his last major Rajput opponent, Rana Pratap of Mewar, in the Battle of Haldighati. (Cannily, he sent the Rajput general Kunwar Man Singh to lead the Mughal army, encouraging his Hindu officers to fight well against another Rajput.) Then, in 1585, he took Kashmir and, in the 1590s, looked to the Deccan, where the Bahmani sultanate had fragmented.

Salim, one of Akbar's three sons, set up his own court at Allahabad in 1600 in what was an understated form of rebellion. But Akbar, perhaps influenced by the women of his harem, remained diplomatic and didn't push Salim into open opposition. When Akbar died in 1605, Salim inherited his empire, taking the name Jahangir, "Conqueror of the World."

Jahangir continued his father's artistic patronage and policy of mixing different religions and cultures. He also accepted the first English ambassador, Sir Thomas Roe, in 1615 and gave him permission for an English "factory" (trading house) at Surat. In his diary, Roe claims that he and the emperor were drinking buddies. However, Jahangir doesn't mention Roe at all in his autobiography.

Like his father Akbar, Jahangir had married a number of Rajput princesses. This tied the Rajput princely houses even more tightly into the Mughal empire. He later married the widow of a Persian officer, Sher Afgan; her name was Nur Jahan, and as Jahangir's twentieth and last wife, she became the power behind the throne, placing members of her family in high offices. She was, apparently, an excellent tiger hunter and keen shot.

Nur Jahan and her father, Mirza Ghiyas Beg (also known by his honorific title of I'timad-ud-Daulah, "Pillar of the State"), became the power behind the throne. Jahangir had inherited Babur's and Akbar's predilections for drugs and alcohol but not their strength of will, so letting Nur Jahan take over much of the business of state was tempting. It also wasn't the worst thing he could have done; Nur Jahan had been well educated by her father and was highly capable as an administrator. She even rescued her husband from captivity when rebels attacked his caravan on the way to Kashmir.

Jahangir died in 1627 without having chosen a successor. Nur Jahan supported prince Shahryar, who had married her daughter Ladli. However, Prince Khurram defeated and executed Shahryar and succeeded to the throne as Shah Jahan ("King of the World"). Nur Jahan spent the rest of her life under house arrest in Lahore.

Shah Jahan is now best remembered as the emperor who built the Taj Mahal for his favorite wife, Mumtaz Mahal. The story of their marriage is one of India's great love stories, but to avoid being too sentimental, it's worth remembering that they had fourteen children, and Mumtaz Mahal died giving birth to the fourteenth. Her body must have been exhausted.

The Taj Mahal, epitome of Mughal architecture and gardening.

© Yann Forget / Wikimedia Commons. https://commons.wikimedia.org/wiki/File:Taj_Mahal_(Edited).jpeg

The Taj Mahal marks the summit of Mughal architecture. While Akbar's architecture was a blend of Indian and Central Asian elements, by Shah Jahan's rule, the two currents had fused into one, and the mausoleum is a completely integrated architectural concept. It uses a rhythmic combination of solids and voids and concave and convex elements, such as the nine open arches in the façade. While on Akbar's mausoleum the little chhatri pavilions all stand separately, the Taj Mahal integrates the four corner domes so they form a pyramidal massing with the main dome.

The pietra dura work of inlaid marble and semiprecious stones is particularly notable, showing naturalistic flowers and making the entire work a reference to the gardens of paradise. All the Mughal emperors from Babur onward loved gardens. The square garden with a building at its center and watercourses for cooling was one of the most delightful contributions of Mughal culture.

After the syncretic and tolerant reigns of the previous two emperors, under Shah Jahan, the Mughal Empire turned back towards Islamic orthodoxy. He also expanded the empire in the south, subduing three of the Deccan sultanates, and defeated a Sikh rebellion in Punjab under Guru Hargobind.

But in 1658, Shah Jahan became seriously ill. He would, in fact, live another seven years, but his illness set off a fratricidal struggle between the crown prince and regent Dara Shukoh and his younger brothers Shuja, Murad Bakhsh, and Aurangzeb. After defeating Dara Shukoh at the Battle of Samugarh, Aurangzeb became the sixth Mughal emperor, declaring his father incompetent to rule and shutting him up in Agra Fort for the rest of his life. (From the fort, Shah Jahan would have seen the Taj Mahal every day, just the other side of the river Yamuna.)

Under Aurangzeb, the Mughal Empire reached its full extent, taking Ladakh (in the Himalayas) as a tributary state and conquering Bengal and the remaining southern sultanates of Bijapur and Golconda (Hyderabad).

However, Aurangzeb finally broke with the Mughal tradition of tolerance. He brought back the jizya, the extra tax on non-Muslims, as well as a super-tax on the profits of Hindu merchants. (He was probably short of funds after the intense warfare preceding his coming to power. However, one result of his policies, and of an increase in land tax, was that many Hindus decided to emigrate to lands under the jurisdiction of the East India Company, where there were no religion-based taxes.)

Aurangzeb also demolished a number of Hindu temples; he was apparently concerned about Muslims who were attracted by Hindu teachings and adopted non-Muslim ways of life or dress. He also executed "heretic" Muslims, such as the Sufi mystic Sarmad Kashani, executed Dara Shukoh on the grounds of apostasy, and had the Sikh Guru Tegh Bahadur put to death.

In particular, Aurengzeb demolished the temple of Vishwanath at Varanasi, and the temple at Mathura, which contained the site of Krishna's birthplace. Some earlier temple destructions can be attributed to the desire of a conqueror to destroy the works of previous rulers. Even some Hindu rulers did this: for instance, Indra III Rashtrakuta destroyed the Pratihara-founded temple at Kalpa. But in the case of Aurangzeb, contemporary documentation shows that his destruction of these temples was motivated purely by religious doctrine. His demolitions of these two important centers of Hindu worship are still a sore point with Hindus today.

But Aurengzeb died a disappointed man. Shivaji and his Marathas were pressing on one side, a Pashtun rebellion in Afghanistan on the other. His interminable wars had impoverished his empire. When he died at the age of 88, he had outlived many of his children and had not appointed a successor.

"I came alone and I go as a stranger," he wrote. "The instant which has passed in power has left only sorrow behind it. I have not been the guardian and protector of the Empire. Life, so valuable, has been squandered in vain. God was in my heart but I could not see him. Life is transient. The past is gone and there is no hope for the future. The whole imperial army is like me: bewildered, perturbed, separated from God, quaking like quicksilver. I fear my punishment. Though I have a firm hope in God's grace, yet for my deeds anxiety ever remains with me" (Dalrymple 2019). His grave, in the little town of Khuldabad, is a simple open-air tomb in the courtyard of a saint's shrine, far from the glories of his predecessors' tombs in Lahore, Delhi, and Agra.

After Aurangzeb's death in 1707, the Mughal state began to crumble. Aurangzeb had damaged the Mughal economy by pursuing an expensive military program; his expansion of the empire came at the expense of its solvency. He had also badly misjudged his sons, expecting them to share the empire among them. (Sharing never seemed to have been a Mughal trait. Aurangzeb should have remembered how he had killed his brothers to ascend to the throne.)

Akbar had ruled 49 years, Jahangir 21, Shah Jahan 30, and Aurangzeb 48. The next emperor, Aurangzeb's third son Azam Shah, ruled for only three months. Bahadur Shah, Aurangzeb's second son, beat Azam Shah in battle and took the throne but died four years later. Bahadur's son Jahandar Shah managed only 350 days before his nephew Farrukhsiyar defeated him in battle, imprisoned him, and then had him strangled.

It was Farrukhsiyar who gave the East India Company a license to trade tax-free in Bengal, Bihar, and Orissa, sowing the seeds of the Mughal Empire's doom. Already, uprisings of Jats, Sikhs, and the Marathas had challenged the empire, and various successor states now began to break away, too; the empire broke down into warring kingdoms. In 1739, the Persians under Nader Shah sacked the capital, Delhi, taking plunder that included Jahangir's Peacock Throne and the Koh-i-Noor diamond.

Between them, Jahangir and Aurangzeb had also managed to turn the Sikhs from peaceful coreligionists into a vengeful army by persecuting the new and relatively small sect. In 1606, Jahangir gave the fifth Sikh guru, Guru Arjan Dev, the choice of converting to Islam or being executed; the guru chose death. After this, Guru Arjan Dev's son and successor as the sixth guru, Guru Hargobind, created a Sikh army. He managed to maintain distant relations with Jahangir, but under Shah Jahan, the Sikhs waged open war against the Mughal Empire and local governors in Punjab. In 1675, Aurangzeb had the ninth Sikh guru, Guru Tegh Bahadur, executed (giving him the same choice Jahangir had given Guru Arjan Dec). After this event, the Sikh identity had been firmly forged not just as a religious but also as a political and military identity.

The Sikhs now depended on their military leaders rather than the gurus. Banda Singh Bahadur headed up the Khalsa (a Sikh community and army) in the early eighteenth century. He abolished the Mughal zamindari tax and land-holding system within Sikh lands, giving peasant farmers ownership of their own land, but he was eventually captured by the Mughals and executed.

After Banda Singh's time, the Sikhs retreated to the jungles and used guerrilla tactics against the Mughals; they were considered little better than bandits by the Mughal Empire. In 1716, Farrukhsiyar commanded that Sikhs, if found, would be either forcibly converted to Islam or executed.

However, by 1783, the battle-hardened Sikhs had turned the tables. Jassa Singh Ramgarhia led a Sikh army into Delhi, and the Mughals under Shah Alam II were forced to make peace. The Sikh Confederacy was now in full control of Punjab. Ranjit Singh, leader of the largest part of the Sikh Confederacy, rose to power as leader of the entire community and, in 1801, was crowned as Maharaja of Punjab, creating the Sikh Empire, which he ruled until his death in 1839.

Maharaja Ranjit Singh, "Lion of the Punjab," from a contemporary portrait.
https://commons.wikimedia.org/wiki/File:Maharaj_Ranjit_Singh.jpg

(After Ranjit Singh's death, however, things fell apart remarkably quickly. There were poisoning, "accidents," assassinations, and four leaders in just two years. Duleep Singh, the last Maharaja, succeeded at the age of five in 1843. He was deposed by the British, then exiled to Britain, where he befriended Queen Victoria, hunted with the Prince of Wales, and was renowned as the fourth best shot in England. His son and successor, Victor Albert Jay Duleep Singh, went to Eton and Sandhurst and married into the British aristocracy; his daughter, Sophia Duleep Singh, became a prominent suffragette, and Catherine Duleep Singh moved to Germany, where she and her former governess helped save a number of Jewish families in the 1930s by helping them move to the UK.)

The late Mughal empire didn't just have the Sikhs to deal with in the north; it was being put under pressure from the south by the late seventeenth century, as well. Shivaji Bhonsle, son of an army officer who had worked for many different local rulers, decided to take advantage of the sultanate of Bijapur's weakness by taking a number of forts for himself. Eventually, Shivaji defeated Bijapur's forces at the Battle of Pratapgarh in 1659 and was then able to take much of the Konkan coast to the west.

Shivaji, with his Maratha followers, invaded the Deccan and headed for Surat in Gujarat. He attacked the Portuguese settlement in Basrur by sea but then had a setback: Aurangzeb's general Jai Singh forced him to a stalemate, and Shivaji signed the Treaty of Purandar, becoming a vassal of the Mughal Empire.

However, Aurangzeb made a bad mistake when he summoned Shivaji to court in 1666: he offended Shivaji by making him stand next to low-ranking men he had defeated in battle. Shivaji protested, refused to come to court again, and was then put under house arrest while Aurangzeb decided what to do with him.

Shivaji, a patient man and a good Hindu, made a practice of sending large baskets of sweets to priests and the poor while he was in prison. After a couple of months of piety, he knew that his jailers were used to seeing the baskets sent out and were no longer paying much attention. He hid in one, his son Sambhaji hid in another, and they were carried stickily to freedom.

Years of uneasy peace with the Mughals followed. Aurengzeb was fighting hard in the north and pulled troops out of the Deccan; many disbanded soldiers decided they would rather join the Marathas. Shivaji had soon retaken the Deccan and most of the coast from Surat nearly all the way down to Goa; eventually, he controlled the peninsula all the way across to Madras. He harassed the English factory in Bombay and invaded Bengal. Finally, he decided that he should be a king. Only one thing stood in his way: the fact that he was Shudra, not Kshatriya, by caste. The Brahmins of his court objected.

Shivaji found a friendly scholar from Varanasi who discovered a genealogy proving he was of royal blood. He was still made to do penance for not observing the correct caste rituals, go through the sacred thread ceremony, and then remarry all his wives according to the Vedic rites. Finally, in 1674, he was crowned king, and the Maratha Empire came into being. Tanjore (Thanjavur), too, came into the empire, then Mysore; the dream of a united south India was very nearly complete.

Shivaji died in 1680 and was succeeded by his sons Sambhaji and Rajaram, then his grandson Shahu. The Marathas very nearly took Delhi itself in 1737, by which time the Mughal Empire had been pushed right back to a small area around Delhi and Panipat, and most of the Muslim states had been conquered. Only the Nizam of Hyderabad had been able to hold out in the south—and would do so until India became independent and beyond.

The Maratha Empire eventually became a confederacy between the Gaekwads of Baroda, the Holkars of Indore and Malwa, the Bhonsales of Nagpur, and the Scindias of Gwalior. For a while, this delicate balancing act seemed to work. Then, suddenly, the British were there, pitting each of these princely families against the others—and the Maratha Empire vanished as quickly as it had come to be. But that's a story that opens a new chapter in India's history.

Chapter 5: Colonial India and the East India Company

The story of the British in India begins with the foundation of the East India Company (EIC or the Company) in 1600. At this time, England was wealthy under Queen Elizabeth I, Shakespeare was writing his plays, and England seemed to be on a roll—except that it had missed out on the wave of wealth coming to Spain and Portugal through the colonization of Latin America. London traders and their seafaring friends wanted something better, and to find it, they looked east, not west.

At first, they concentrated on setting up trading stations, known as "factories," enabling them to export Indian goods such as palampores (highly decorated cloth), cotton, silk, and indigo. (The Dutch had already taken control of the spice trade, concentrating on Indonesia.) In the early seventeenth century, trade was set up at Machilipatnam/Masulipatnam on the east coast, Surat in Gujarat, Burhampore and Cossimbazar in Bengal, Calicut/Kozhikode in Kerala, Patna, Madras/Chennai, and Dacca/Dhaka (now the capital of Bangladesh); in the later seventeenth century, Hooghly, Bombay/Mumbai, and Calcutta followed.

The EIC started small but grew rapidly. By 1750, the EIC made up nearly £1 million of Britain's total £8 million import trade, tea alone accounting for £0.5 million of revenue. Many Members of Parliament (MPs) and members of the House of Lords were shareholders in the EIC, so it had become, as it were, the tail that wagged the dog. If it needed legislation passed to support its aims, it had many "tame" MPs who would support it.

Even so, the EIC was simply a business investment company, an import/export business, so to speak. However, two major trends would eventually change the status of British involvement in India. The first was the gradual breakdown of the Mughal Empire. The second was the increasing tension between France and Britain, which became a global conflict fought out through the American War of Independence and in India.

The Carnatic Wars from 1746 to 1763 were sparked off by the War of the Austrian Succession in Europe. (This set France, Prussia, and Spain against the Habsburg monarchy and Britain, eventually involving most of Europe.)

Joseph François Dupleix, governor of the French East India Company, was an ambitious man and saw how he could expand French influence in India by attacking the British. While at first successful, he came up against the young Robert Clive.

Clive appears to have been something of a thug as a youngster. He was a troublemaker at school, always fighting, and his father may have sent him out to India because he simply didn't know what to do with him. He became a remarkably brave (even foolhardy) Company officer, though he had no military training—his first two years were spent mainly keeping the Company's accounts in Fort St. George (Madras). He was involved in the First Carnatic War when, in 1746, Madras was seized and the Company's officers taken to Pondicherry as captives. He managed to escape with three others dressed as Indians; later, he was given a platoon at the Siege of Pondicherry, where he distinguished himself in action.

In 1748, the death of the Nizam of Hyderabad set off the Second Carnatic War. Here, Clive really made his name, making several forced marches to take the fort of Arcot by surprise. When he was surrounded by besiegers, he waited for night and launched a surprise attack on the other army; they fled, never finding out how small his forces were. Surprise had become one of Clive's signature tactics. Eventually, French India was reduced to the single outpost of Pondicherry (where the bakers still serve excellent croissants and the policemen wear French-style képis).

Despite now being called "Clive of India" by the British public, Clive actually loathed India and was glad of the chance to retire to England, having made his fortune. He spent the next couple of years playing

British politics—and losing. However, he was called back to India, and since he appears to have already spent a significant part of his fortune, he may have needed to take up his post again to receive fresh funds. He landed in Madras but, following the news that Cossimbazar and Calcutta had been taken by the Nawab of Bengal, was quickly sent north to deal with the situation.

Mughal Bengal was ruled from Murshidabad and had allowed numerous factories to be set up along the Hooghly River by the Portuguese, Dutch, and Armenians, as well as the English. This was, at the time, one of the richest areas of India, with a huge textile trade, and the Nawabs had created a courtly culture of some sophistication. The provinces of Bihar, Bengal, and Orissa (from 1741) were ruled by Nawab Alivardi Khan, who maintained strict neutrality with the European nations that traded in Bengal; unlike the south, Bengal had escaped involvement in the wars between France and Britain. (Alivardi was a cat-lover and often did business with a white Persian cat on his lap—a Mughal version of the James Bond series' Ernest Blofeld!)

For finance, Alivardi also relied on the Seth family of bankers. They acted as the central treasury, and controlled the mint selling currency to the EIC and making a commission on this supply. The Seth bank had branches in several Company towns, such as Calcutta, Surat, Bombay, and Madras.

However, Alivardi died in 1756, and his successor, his 23-year-old nephew Siraj ud-Daulah, did not follow Alivardi's cautious policies. He has often been dismissed as a drunkard and even presented as a serial bisexual rapist and psychopath (Dalrymple, 2019). Siraj had made himself persona non grata with the British through his intemperate behavior and, determined to teach them a lesson, marched on first on Cossimbazar and then Calcutta.

The British were overwhelmed; Fort William was not well-equipped, and the governor, Roger Drake, decided to flee with a number of officers. A surgeon, John Holwell, took command of the men who were left and formally surrendered to Siraj ud-Daulah. At first, the men were well treated, but after a few soldiers got drunk and started making themselves obnoxious, the British were rounded up and put into the prison of their own fort, the famous "Black Hole of Calcutta." The night was one of the hottest of the year, and after a night packed into the small room without water or fresh air, many of the men suffocated.

The Black Hole was not particularly celebrated at the time, but in Victorian India, it became a classic symbol of Indian barbarity and backwardness. However, it is worth remembering that the Black Hole was created by the British, and they thought it perfectly adequate for holding prisoners—although perhaps not in such high numbers. In recent years, the numbers cited by Holwell have also been challenged. According to him, only 23 of 146 people forced into the cell survived the night, but other historians have assessed the number of prisoners at the much lower 64 and 43.

One Bengali historian decided to take an experimental approach, marking off a square the same size as the cell, 18 square feet. He then asked local villagers to fill the space. Even though the Bengali villagers were probably smaller and thinner than the British soldiers had been and pushed as tightly together as possible, he could not manage to get 146 of them into the space.

Had Siraj ud-Daulah only upset the British, he might have survived. But he also upset the Jagat Seth ("Banker of the World") Mahtab Rai, his treasurer. When he couldn't get enough money out of the treasury, he slapped the Seth in public, making a formidable enemy of his main financier. He also replaced his paymaster, Mir Jafar. That was unwise; the Seths then decided they would work secretly for the British, and Mir Jafar joined the conspiracy. (He also had his eyes on the Nawab's throne.)

Clive quickly managed to retake Calcutta. Then, he took the French enclave of Chandannagar and declared war on Siraj ud-Daulah, marching his army up the Hooghly River toward Murshidabad. At Plassey, he found the Nawab's army already entrenched, with reinforcements expected to arrive in two days. Clive had his army take up position in a mango grove near a hunting lodge. His army was hugely outnumbered and tired, having crossed the river in spate to get to Plassey.

Siraj ud-Daulah's army was big, but Clive had a secret advantage. Mir Jafar, who led a large part of Siraj ud-Daulah's army, had pledged that his troops would not engage in the fight, but he would keep them standing by. He had also bribed other officers in the Bengali army. Everything hinged on whether Clive's allies in the Bengali camp would keep their word.

At daybreak on June 23, 1757, Siraj's artillery opened fire. The barrage continued all morning, but Siraj did not charge. After half an hour, Clive moved his men into the mango grove, which was protected by an embankment from the worst of the shelling. Mir Jafar was there with his division of the army but had not actively engaged in the battle. (Was he just biding his time or actively helping the English?)

At noon, it started to rain. Siraj had taken no precautions against the rain, and his artillery found its ammunition had gotten wet and would not fire. Meanwhile, Clive, who had not started to fire until now, and whose artillery was well-protected by tarpaulins, was able to commence continuous fire on the Nawab's army.

At this point, Mir Madan, the Bengali artillery chief, decided to attack the British, leading the charge on his war elephant. Thanks to a sharp-shooting Company soldier, Mir Madan was shot and carried to the Nawab's tent, where he died. This turned the course of the battle; Siraj ud-Daulah seems to have lost all confidence and decided to retreat. Finally, Mir Jafar's men marched away, leaving Clive the victor.

Plassey cost the Nawab 500 men, including some of his best officers, such as Mir Madan, and three elephants. Only 22 British soldiers died, though 50 were wounded. Plassey opened the way to Murshidabad, where Mir Jafar had Siraj ud-Daulah murdered and then took power.

If Siraj had won the battle of Plassey, the EIC in Bengal would have been wiped out (and so would Mir Jafar, most likely). It was a desperate throw of the dice by Clive, but it worked. The Company was no longer just a trading house but a regional power in India. It was Clive, and not the Mughal emperor, who authorized Mir Jafar's coronation as Nawab. As a result, it was a multinational corporation and not the Mughal Empire that held political power. Bengal had effectively submitted to a corporate takeover.

In the future, the Company would continue to work through "tame" local rulers. For instance, in 1765, Sir Hector Munro defeated Shuja ud-Daulah, the Nawab of Awadh (Oudh), at Buxar; Clive reinstalled him as a "tame" Nawab, and Awadh remained a close ally of the Company for over a century. (Incidentally, Clive enriched himself by what we'd now call insider trading. When he heard of the victory at Buxar, he ordered his agent in England to mortgage his house and invest the funds in Company shares. He must have made a fortune on the deal.) The capture of Awadh gave the British huge leverage over the Mughals. The emperor, Shah Alam II, was prevailed upon to give the British the diwani rights to Bengal, Bihar, and Orissa, effectively making them governors of the province and giving them the right to collect tax revenue.

Clive returned to Britain as one of the richest men in the country, but he was not a happy man, and in 1774, he cut his throat with a penknife. He was only 49.

Bengal saw miserable times following the battle of Plassey. Clive's gamble had been costly, and the Company needed to gain a return on its investment. The easiest way of doing so was not through trade but by taxation. Bengal was bled white.

Unfortunately, by 1769, climatic conditions were changing. There was no rainfall; without rain, rice became short. By the end of 1770, famine had killed as many as ten million, a third of the population. Unlike Indian rulers, the British had not set up strategic rice reserves or charitable distribution networks. The Company's huge debts still had to be serviced, while the famine meant no tax revenues were coming in. Having killed millions of Indians, the Company managed to nearly kill itself: by 1773, it had to be bailed out by the British government.

Clive had identified several gifted men within the Company. One of these was Warren Hastings, whom Clive had made the British resident at Murshidabad. Hastings was very different from Clive; he was a scholar and a diligent manager, and he fell in love with India, quickly learning Persian, Urdu, and later Bengali. He also made a number of reforms. Clive had already created a modern army for the EIC, but Hastings transformed its bureaucracy and improved British knowledge about the subcontinent. He codified the laws, started the cartographical survey of India, and created a postal service. He also founded the Asiatic Society and sponsored a translation of the Bhagavad Gita. And he built huge granaries, including the immense Golghar in Patna (which can still be seen today), to avoid any future famine becoming as bad as the one in 1769-70.

Warren Hastings, painted by Tilly Kettle. This pensive and unassuming man ran India, and his second wife was a German baroness.

https://commons.wikimedia.org/wiki/File:Warren_Hastings_by_Tilly_Kettle.jpg

In 1773, Madras, Bombay, and Calcutta were brought under unified control with Hastings' appointment as governor-general; the Company became a single power rather than a trio of separate enclaves. Having been bailed out by the British government, it had also, in some sense, been nationalized. Though it retained autonomy, the government could now pull the strings.

Bengal and northern India were pretty much under British control, or at least influence, by now; this made the next major area for British expansion the south, where Haidar Ali and his son Tipu Sultan of Mysore formed a determined opposition to the Company. Haidar Ali had adopted modern military techniques from the French army in India, so his kingdom was not an easy conquest. In fact, there appears to have been a Jacobin club of French Republican officers in Mysore; Tipu is said to have planted a tree of liberty and declared himself "Citizen Tipu"—though this latter event may have been Company propaganda.

For a long time, the Mysore Sultans successful stopped the British, but in 1792, General Lord Cornwallis finally managed to take Bangalore. Even so, he could not take Tipu's fortress at Srirangapatna. Tipu still had to surrender, ceding half his territory.

Things were left to rest for a while, but once again, European events dictated the course of events in India: Nelson's victory at the Battle of Trafalgar in 1798 deprived Tipu of potential further French support, and Marquess Wellesley, with his brother Arthur (later the Duke of

Wellington) on his staff, decided to go on the offensive now that Tipu was isolated. They took Srirangapatna on May 4, 1799, after a siege of nearly a month. Tipu, a fighter to the last, was killed defending the walls of his fort.

One small but intriguing souvenir of Tipu's court can now be found in the Victoria and Albert Museum in London—Tipu's tiger. The tiger was the emblem of Tipu's dynasty. His men wore tiger-striped tunics, there were tiger stripes on his coins, and his throne had tiger-headed arms. This beautifully carved and painted wooden tiger is shown in the act of killing an East India Company soldier, whose dying moans are imitated by the pipe organ hidden inside the tiger.

The Scindias and the Holkars were now the last remnants of the Maratha Empire, the Holkars ruling from Indore and the Scindias in Ujjain and later in Gwalior. Yashwantrao Holkar tried but failed to unite the remaining Maratha rulers and was ultimately prevailed upon to sign the Treaty of Rajghat in 1805, recognizing him as sovereign king but allying him with the British.

The Third Anglo-Maratha War in 1818 saw the conquest of the remaining Marathas, after which Indore and Gwalior became princely states under British rule. Bundelkhand, most of Rajasthan, and Nagpur all became British territories at the same time. Over the years, British India expanded its scope through alliances with states such as Cochin, Travancore (now Kerala), and Hyderabad. The East India Company had started as several tiny, isolated islands within India; now, it controlled — whether by conquest or alliance—virtually the whole subcontinent.

At the same time, the nature of British involvement in India was changing. Previously, many British Company employees had settled in India, marrying Indian women and often living the life of an Indian noble. Cornwallis put an end to that: he decreed that the British were not to settle in India. They became an expatriate community, returning to Britain after their tours of duty. This automatically downgraded the status of Anglo-Indian families. It also led to a wider social barrier between the British and the Indians; British clubs and social networks excluded Indians. The governor-general and later viceroy, for instance, was always a temporary appointment, normally a five-year term; the longest-serving was Lord Linlithgow, with just eight years of total service. Many Viceroys had not visited India before their appointment and consequently often had a poor understanding of the country they ruled.

Cornwallis also carried out land reforms that started to change the social makeup of India. His land reforms ruined many old Mughal families, and the Hindu bhadraloks (equivalent to "gentlemen") emerged to fill their place.

Cornwallis' intention with his various changes was probably to avoid India becoming like America, where English settlers had become more attached to America than their country of origin. However, his reforms led to India being administered by men who had no long-term interest in, or love for, the country.

The Company remained in control until 1857, although it was increasingly influenced by the British government's priorities. However, 1857 was a traumatic year and marked a decisive change in the nature of British rule. This was the year of what earlier British historians call the Sepoy Rebellion (Indian soldiers in the Company army were known as sepoys) but is now more frequently referred to as the Indian Rebellion of 1857; it can also be seen as the first war of independence.

There were many reasons for the rebellion. High taxes, reforms such as banning sati (widows joining their husbands on the funeral pyre), and rumors of forced conversions to Christianity had all alienated Indians. The Doctrine of Lapse, which allowed the British to take over princely states without a direct heir, was another sore point. And the Bengal army, recruited mainly from the higher castes, had grievances, such as being expected to serve overseas without the traditional special overseas payment.

The immediate spark for the rebellion was the introduction of the new Enfield rifle. This rifle used ready-prepared cartridges wrapped in greased paper; the end of the cartridge had to be bitten off before inserting it into the gun. The soldiers of the Bengal Army based at Meerut, near Delhi, heard that the cartridges were greased with beef tallow (forbidden to Hindus) and pork lard (forbidden to Muslims). Several soldiers based there refused to accept the cartridges; they were court-martialed and imprisoned.

The next day, the Indian troops revolted, freeing their imprisoned colleagues and killing several British officers and civilians. They then made for Delhi, where they called on the Mughal emperor, Bahadur Shah, to lead them against the British. Initially unwilling, at last he was compelled to accept. (This probably ensured that the Sikhs, who well remembered their persecution under Shah Jahan and Aurangzeb, remained on the side of the British.) The British marched on Delhi, besieging the city for nearly three months before taking it. Bahadur Shah was arrested, two of his sons and his grandson Mirza Abu Bakr were shot, and the Mughal Empire was brought to an end with Bahadur Shah's exile to Burma.

The rebellion saw a huge scale of violence and retribution. At Kanpur/Cawnpore, the British in the town were besieged for three weeks; Nana Sahib, leader of the revolt, offered General Wheeler a chance to escape by boat down the Ganges to Allahabad. The dock was surrounded by Indian troops who opened fire once most of the British had arrived. This may well have been by accident. Nana Sahib took the women and children who had survived to the Bibighar, the home of the local magistrate's clerk. However, once it was clear that the British were winning and Nana Sahib could not hold out, he ordered the massacre of all survivors. For Victorian Britons, this event symbolized the Indians' barbarity and wickedness—just like the Black Hole of Calcutta—and was used to justify reprisals.

The British eventually put down the rebellion, but the East India Company's days were numbered. The Government of India Act 1858 formally dissolved the Company and transferred its rule over India to the British government. The Company had outlasted the Mughal Empire by only a year.

Under the British Raj, Queen Victoria was installed as Empress of India, and many changes took place within India. Some of these were the disbanding of the old Bengal Army regiments and the decision to recruit primarily from among the Sikhs, Baluchis, and Gurkhas, who had either supported the British or not been involved in the revolt. Maharajas and large landholders, who had mostly refused to support the revolt, were rewarded by having their territories guaranteed; no more land reforms would be carried out for nearly a century.

The Industrial Revolution had already impacted India, but this accelerated. Railways were built throughout India, with new roads, bridges, and even canals—though these were intended to benefit the import and export trades in British control rather than Indian interests. Nonetheless, the coming of the railway created a vast infrastructure that has had a huge influence on Indian life. Many Indians migrate across the subcontinent to work in the big cities, while it's not unusual for a student to take a full-day train journey to attend one of the best-reputed universities or technical institutes. (Mahatma Gandhi always traveled third class to meet the ordinary people of India and even wrote a book entitled Third Class in Indian Railways.)

The railways also created a huge source of employment; Anglo-Indians, in particular, formed a large community of railway employees. Indian Railways now employ 1.3 million people and is introducing a new generation of super-fast trains, such as the Shatabdi Express.

CST Terminal, Mumbai—the railways in Indo-Saracenic style.

Usernamekiran, CC BY-SA 4.0 <https://creativecommons.org/licenses/by-sa/4.0>, via Wikimedia Commons; https://commons.wikimedia.org/wiki/File:Chhatrapati_Shivaji_Terminus_railway_station_(cropped).jpg

Although Indians were still second-class citizens in their own country, education opened new opportunities. By the late nineteenth century, some Indians started studying in England, often gaining legal qualifications. The fathers of Independence were mostly London-educated barristers (today, they would be more likely to have been educated at Harvard or MIT).

There is no doubt among modern historians that the Raj drained India of wealth just as effectively as the Company had done. Even John Sullivan, the Company's Collector at Coimbatore, admitted how little Company rule did for India: "The little court disappears—trade languishes—the capital decays—the people are impoverished—the Englishman flourishes, and acts like a sponge, drawing up riches from the banks of the Ganges, and squeezing them down upon the banks of the Thames" (cited in Tharoor, Inglorious Empire, Ch. 1).

In the eighteenth century, India had exported finished materials to Europe. Under the Raj, it was prevented from competing with British industry and became a provider of raw materials instead; in fact, Britain started exporting cloth *to* India. The railways imported their locomotives from Britain, and the Indian taxpayer paid for them. No wonder that by the early twentieth century, Indians were beginning to think about independence.

Chapter 6: Gandhi: Freedom and Partition

The story of Indian independence is not just the story of Gandhi, but it is impossible to imagine independence coming about the way it did without Gandhi's involvement. Gandhi is, to many, the face of independence. Every city in India has an MG road named after him, and the country's banknotes feature Gandhi's face, with his trademark round spectacles.

Gandhi shown on a 5-rupee banknote, with an Ashoka column in the bottom left corner.
Reserve Bank of India / AKS.9955, CC BY-SA 4.0 <https://creativecommons.org/licenses/by-sa/4.0>, via Wikimedia Commons; https://commons.wikimedia.org/wiki/File:5_Rupees_%28Obverse%29.jpg

Born in Porbandar, Gujarat, where his father was chief minister, Gandhi studied as a lawyer at the Inner Temple, London. Even then, his principles and his methods of social action were becoming clear: he was involved in supporting a dockers' strike and joined the London

Vegetarian Society. In 1893, he moved to South Africa (another British colony), practicing law there for twenty-one years.

It was in South Africa that he saw racial discrimination first-hand. He'd considered himself "a Briton first and an Indian second" (Herman, 87). But when he moved to South Africa, he discovered that his skin made him an Indian first and was subject to many, often humiliating, restrictions.

Gandhi founded the Natal Indian Congress and began to create a coherent Indian political voice in South Africa; he also worked as ambulance corps and stretcher-bearer in the Boer War and the Zulu Revolt. In 1914, he found himself aboard a ship for London when the First World War broke out. When he arrived, he organized a volunteer ambulance corps whose members were mainly Indian students in London and took nursing classes.

In 1915, he returned to India and started working for civil rights. For instance, in 1917, he assisted peasants growing indigo in Bihar but not receiving adequate pay; he won significant concessions for them. In 1918, when Kheda was hit by floods, he organized a social boycott of tax officials using non-cooperation to achieve his arms. Eventually, the government gave way, suspending taxes for 1918 and 1919.

Gandhi often worked with the lowest classes, and his vision for independence was resolutely Indian. Earlier nationalists, for instance in Bengal, had often looked to English institutions as a way forward and got much of their support from the growing Indian middle class. Gandhi not only worked with the workers and farmers but also reclaimed Indian traditions, becoming an Indian leader visibly with his decision to wear traditional clothing rather than the western suit.

The end of the First World War brought disillusionment for many Indians. Many of the Indian regiments had fought in the war, in France or at Gallipoli, and had expected to be given increasing democracy as a result. Britain gave them nothing. In fact, they got worse than nothing, as the Rowlatt Act of 1919 was passed to block "terrorist" nationalist activities. Among other things, it allowed indefinite detention without trial.

By 1921, Gandhi had become the leader of the Indian National Congress and introduced the concept of satyagraha. His advocacy of non-violent action may seem impractical, but Gandhi considered it the only pragmatically effective way to protest. "The British want to put us on the plane of machine guns where they have the weapons and we do not. Our only assurance of beating them is putting the struggle on a plane where we have the weapons and they have not" (cited in Shirer, Ch. 1). There was nothing New Age or wishy-washy about Gandhi's tactics; he realized that the British were only able to impose the Raj through the cooperation of their Indian subjects. If the Indians stopped cooperating, British rule would—eventually—collapse.

Protest against the Rowlatt Act was particularly strong in Punjab, where General Dyer decided to impose martial law. He banned all meetings, but—most likely in ignorance rather than defiance of his edict—many villagers met in the garden of Jallianwala Bagh at Amritsar to celebrate the Sikh and Hindu festival of Vaisakhi. The crowd was estimated at about 6,000 (but may well have been more) in a park with only five entrances through narrow, lockable gates.

No order was given to the crowd to disperse. Instead, Dyer blocked the exits, then ordered his troops to fire into the garden. Firing continued for ten minutes. The number of casualties is disputed. The Times of India gave a figure of 200 killed the day after; the Hunter Commission set up by the governor-general estimated 400 deaths, including a six-week-old baby; and the Indian National Congress investigation gave a figure of 1,000 dead and 500 wounded.

Jallianwala Bagh was a turning point for many moderate Indians, including Gandhi; this appears to have been the point at which he finally lost faith in British promises of democracy within the Raj. Rabindranath Tagore, winner of the Nobel Prize for literature, renounced his British knighthood as an act of protest.

Worse, a few days later, General Dyer forced Indians in Amritsar's Kucha Kurrichhan street to crawl on their hands and knees. The "crawling order" was meant to humiliate, and it did, but it also showed many Indians that the British would never treat them as equals. Even more galling, Britain's Morning Post raised over £26,000 for Dyer's benefit.

Calls for swaraj, full independence, continued. Gandhi now advocated a policy of swadeshi, boycotting British-made goods. He clearly understood the economic underpinnings of colonialism. In 1930, he led the Salt March to Dandi, a march of 250 miles to protest the British imposition of tax on salt. He vowed that when he arrived at the sea, he would make his own salt, thus breaking the law.

At first, the action was considered by the British (and some Indians) to be a mere joke, but in fact, Gandhi had found a powerful symbol. One hundred people started the march, but thousands joined along the way. (Gandhi himself compared it to the Boston Tea Party.)

In 1931, Lord Irwin, governor-general of India, made an agreement with Gandhi to hold a Round Table Conference in London to discuss the Congress' demands. Many members of the Congress, like Jawaharlal Nehru, believed Gandhi had conceded too much. However, what the British had conceded was the principle of independence. Gandhi saw this; the British did not.

Congress' demanded the complete independence of India, with Indian control of the army, foreign policy, and economic policy; an impartial tribunal to determine the division of the national debt between India and Britain; and the right of India to secede from the British Empire at any stage.

The Round Table was packed with representatives who had been picked by the British; they made attempts to split off the Muslims, lower castes and Untouchables, and the Anglo-Indians by offering them special status. However, Gandhi made a tough and very sharp negotiator. For instance, in his argument on the division of the national debt, he asserted that British expenditure in India had been for British purposes, and therefore India should not be required to pay any of that debt. Eventually, the talks were abandoned.

While he was in Britain, Gandhi visited Lancashire mill workers, who had seen their jobs threatened as swadeshi impacted textile exports to India. They admired his grasp of the cotton business—which was not surprising since this was the main business of Ahmedabad, where he had led the first big strike against mill owners in India. Later, Gandhi told Shirer that their technology was backward; that was why they couldn't compete, and swadeshi had nothing to do with it (Shirer Ch. 11).

Throughout the 1930s, satyagraha continued. The British arrested Congress leaders and continued to try to "divide and rule," for instance suggesting separate electorates for Untouchables and Muslims. In 1935, the Government of India Act introduced a limited franchise. However, the act did not go far enough for Congress. By giving representation to Indian rulers of the princely states and giving every minority the right to vote for candidates from their own community, the act was intended to ensure that Congress could not achieve an outright majority. The act also reserved control of the Indian Army and Treasury and ensured that governors appointed by the UK retained important powers.

When the Second World War broke out in 1939, Gandhi opposed providing help to the British war effort. His point was a principled one: India, he said, could not fight a "war for democracy" while at the same time being denied its own freedom. In 1942, Gandhi launched the Quit India Movement. He was now in his seventies, but it was time, he said, to "Do or Die" (Karo ya Maro). Within hours, the leadership of Congress had been jailed without trial.

Two and a half million Indians joined the British force, nonetheless.

Perhaps this was a mistake. Congress leaders remained cooped up for most of the war, and this made it easier for Mohammed Ali Jinnah, leader of the All-India Muslim League, to secure concessions. If Congress had taken a softer line, the leaders would have kept in touch with the masses and with the British, and the arrangements made at independence might have been very different.

In February 1943, Gandhi began a fast to the death. Winston Churchill, the British prime minister and a firm opponent of Indian independence, ordered the Viceroy to let him starve; it was only owing to pressure from his Cabinet that he finally gave in. Gandhi's wife, Kasturba, died while they were still interned.

Gandhi's great failure was that he was unable to win the Muslims over. He wanted a pluralist India for Muslims and Hindus alike, but the Muslim League leadership increasingly backed a separate electorate and, in the end, a separate state. Thus, when India was finally granted independence by the Attlee government in 1947, Pakistan (including what is now Bangladesh, as East Pakistan) was separated from India.

Instead of celebrating, Gandhi spent Independence Day spinning, fasting, and praying for peace.

Gandhi's prayers were not answered. Partition led to large-scale violence between Muslims and Hindus; fifteen million people were displaced, and a million were killed. Even today, Pakistan and India have a very uneasy relationship, having fought four full-scale wars and experienced numerous border skirmishes.

Not all Hindus approved of Gandhi, either; many felt that he had been too generous to Muslims. And so, he outlived independence by just six months. On January 30, 1948, a Hindu militant, Nathuram Godse, assassinated Gandhi as he came out to address a prayer meeting.

It was the end of an era. Jawaharlal Nehru, now Prime Minister of India, addressed the country over All-India Radio:

"Friends and comrades, the light has gone out of our lives, and there is darkness everywhere, and I do not quite know what to tell you or how to say it. Our beloved leader, Bapu as we called him, the father of the nation, is no more. Perhaps I am wrong to say that; nevertheless, we will not see him again, as we have seen him for these many years, we will not run to him for advice or seek solace from him, and that is a terrible blow, not only for me, but for millions and millions in this country."

(Cited in Collins and Lapierre, Freedom at Midnight, 75.)

Chapter 7: The Indian Republic

Gandhi was instrumental in gaining independence for India and was a symbol of the struggle to find an authentically Indian existence for the nation. But he wasn't the only one working for independence, and his ideas were not shared by all his colleagues. And, of course, the idea of independence started well before Gandhi's birth—to the 1857 rebellion, in fact.

The 1857 rebellion did not start as a demand for independence but as a local mutiny. However, as the rebellion developed, it became a national revolt. For many in the independence movement, it was a defining historical moment, showing that India was capable of fighting for its rights. The later nineteenth century was a period of increasing political awareness for Indians, culminating in the foundation of the Indian National Congress in 1885.

The Indian National Congress was sparked by an idea from a Briton, retired civil servant and ornithologist Allan Octavian Hume. He believed that British rule had failed due to its contempt for Indians and aimed to create a vehicle through which Indians could express their desire for progress. At first, most of the members of Congress were made up of the western-educated elite—lawyers, journalists, and teachers—and Congress' political activity was restricted to submitting resolutions on civil rights to the Indian government, which appears not to have believed most of them worth considering. Still, Congress gave Indians a communal political voice and gave them that voice as Indians, regardless of their religion, class, caste, or place of residence.

Progress is never simple, and a huge wrench was thrown in the works by Lord Curzon, appointed viceroy of India in 1899. He was unusually sympathetic to Indian culture and the Indian people; he had traveled across Asia and the Middle East, giving him a feel for non-European societies and cultures—quite unusual in a viceroy. He restored the Taj Mahal and the tomb of Emperor Akbar at Sikandra; he also determined that crimes committed by Britons against Indians should be more severely punished. (Formerly, there was a legal double standard that punished Indians more severely than the British for crimes against members of the other race.) Curzon saw the importance of India to British economic and political power and aimed to tie the Raj even more securely to the UK.

So, it is ironic that Curzon was responsible for an act that gave new impetus to the desire for independence and also started to drive a wedge between the Muslim and Hindu independence movements. His partition of Bengal in 1905 was one of the worst things he could possibly have done.

Bengal was India's largest province by far. It included today's states of Bihar, parts of Orissa and Assam, as well as what is now Bangladesh; administering such a large state was a difficult job. Curzon's intention was simply to reduce the tasks of administration to a scale that was easier to handle, but he appears not to have really understood the political sensitivity of his decision.

By splitting the state into East and West Bengal, he was also splitting it into a Muslim-majority state and a Hindu-majority state, respectively. This reflected the "divide and rule" tactics of the Raj even if that was not his intention. He was also reducing Hindu Bengalis to a minority within West Bengal, which they had to share with Oriya and Maithili speakers. Many Hindu Bengalis—particularly the English-educated middle classes of Calcutta—saw this as an attack on their influence.

The partition of Bengal immediately triggered a nationalist reaction. In 1911, it was unwound; Bihar and Orissa became a new province, and Bengal was reunited. However, Curzon's damage could not be undone. The Muslims of East Bengal, having had their own province for six years, now felt let down, and this resentment led many Muslims toward the idea of separate electorates to safeguard their rights. Although Congress espoused the idea of a secular, multi-faith India, it was increasingly seen as a Hindu party, and the All-India Muslim League, established in

Dhaka in 1906, became increasingly powerful.

Congress was largely a moderate party, espousing change within British institutions. However, a less moderate wing of the party shared the views of Congress member Bal Gangadhar Tilak, that "Swaraj [independence] is my birthright and I shall have it!" Congress eventually expelled Tilak, but his views on using boycotts to damage British rule influenced Gandhi and many others; outside Congress, his message found other listeners.

While Gandhi's place as the hero of the independence struggle gives the impression that Indian nationalism was generally pacifist, there were many Indians who did not agree. Revolutionaries such as Khudiram Bose made a number of attacks on British officers in Bengal; the paramilitary Jugantar organization, associated with the Communist Party, carried out several bomb attacks and even attempted to assassinate the viceroy during a ceremonial procession in 1912 (managing to kill his mahout, while the viceroy and his wife escaped).

As mentioned previously, the desire for independence did not prevent India from supporting Britain in the First World War. Over a million Indians served in the war effort; Sikhs and Pathans (Pashtuns) fought in Northern France. However, after the war was over, British measures to give a limited amount of local power-sharing left the Indians dissatisfied. Many Indians had believed they would receive significant progress towards independence in reward for their assistance in the war, and being given representatives whose decisions could be overruled by the viceroy was not, in their view, real democracy or independence.

So, in 1920, it was in an environment of widespread discontent that Gandhi started the non-cooperation movement. It was also under his influence that Congress moved from being an elite political club to a mass movement. Gandhi was the visionary, but he had assistance from a relatively little-known creator of independence, Vallabhbhai Patel, his "fixer." Patel was the only one of the major players who had risen from the mass of the people; he had worked in the textile mills of Ahmedabad to pay for his education, then qualified as a lawyer. He gave his successful practice up to support Gandhi in the fight against extortionate taxes at flood-hit Kheda and continued to support Gandhi's political aims thereafter. Patel was a gifted organizer, raising funds and bringing people into the party; after independence, he set up the Indian Civil Service.

Jawaharlal Nehru, a Cambridge-educated lawyer, was more Westernized in his outlook than Gandhi. He became the leader of a progressive faction of Congress in the 1920s and did not always agree with Gandhi; in particular, he thought India should have supported the Allied war effort in 1939. Despite these disagreements, Gandhi saw Nehru as his political successor, and it was Nehru who became India's first prime minister. As PM, he promoted science and technology, setting India on the path it follows today as a regional powerhouse of technology. His speech in Congress on the day before Independence Day shows the fervor and optimism of the time:

"Long years ago we made a tryst with destiny, and now the time comes when we shall redeem our pledge, not wholly or in full measure, but very substantially. At the stroke of the midnight hour, when the world sleeps, India will awake to life and freedom. A moment comes, which comes but rarely in history, when we step out from the old to the new, when an age ends, and when the soul of a nation long suppressed finds utterance."

Perhaps the most ambiguous figure in the fight for independence is Subhas Chandra Bose, or Netaji ("Honored Leader"). Bose was Nehru's successor as Congress leader in 1938, but he was not fully in sympathy with Gandhi's ideals of nonviolence and resigned, leaving the party. Subsequently, he attempted to gain support from Nazi Germany for a Free India Legion and then joined the Japanese, creating the Indian National Army (INA). He died when his plane crashed in Taiwan in 1945; his army had already been wiped out.

Views of Bose differ. Some Hindutva nationalists have tried to claim him as a hero; other Indians are embarrassed by what they consider his betrayal of Congress ideals.

Muhammad Ali Jinnah, another London-trained lawyer, was the longtime leader of the All-India Muslim League. He was also a member of Congress until 1920 when he resigned because he could not support the satyagraha campaign. As a thoroughly Westernized individual, he was also suspicious of Gandhi's "Hindu fads" and appeal to the masses, believing the educated elite should lead India to independence.

Gradually, Jinnah came to believe that India's Muslims needed their own state to avoid becoming marginalized in a Hindu nation. He also began to rediscover his Muslim roots; the breakup of his marriage may also have made him more introspective and perhaps turned him toward a new Muslim identity. Having created the country's partition, naturally, he is not celebrated in modern India, but he is regarded as the father of modern Pakistan, of which he became the first governor-general. Like Gandhi, he did not enjoy independence for long, dying just a year after leading his country to independence.

Winston Churchill had always been an opponent of Indian independence, but the election of Clement Attlee as British Prime Minister in 1945 opened the way to swaraj. Together with the new viceroy, Admiral Lord Louis Mountbatten, he took two years to negotiate the detailed provisions for Indian independence. However, partitioning the country into largely Hindu India and mainly Muslim Pakistan was part of the agreement. Gandhi remained true to his view that India should be a single, pluralist, secular state, but Nehru and Patel disagreed. In August 1947, two separate countries were brought into being. (Pakistan was created at midnight on the 14th and India on the 15th.)

Throughout the history of the Company and the Raj, the British had employed "divide and rule tactics," which had already led to sporadic outbreaks of Hindu-Muslim violence. Hindu purity rules also created a barrier between the communities; in some villages, separate wells were provided for each religion, as high-caste Hindus would not even drink from the same water as Muslims. Partition became a bloodbath, and this led to an increased perception that Hindus were only safe with other Hindus and Muslims with other Muslims.

There were 565 officially-recognized princely states at independence, and they were given the choice of which country they would join. For a long time, the rajas and maharajas retained their privy purse payments and their luxurious lifestyles. The Nizam of Hyderabad, however, refused to join either Pakistan or India; this was a tricky situation, as he was a Muslim ruler of a majority-Hindu state, already facing the Communist-led Telangana Rebellion. In 1948, India invaded in "Operation Polo," a five-day strike that led to the resignation of the Nizam and the integration of Hyderabad into India. A further accession followed with the integration of the Kingdom of Sikkim in 1975.

The princely families continued a life of ease but little political power until 1971 when they were finally pensioned off in the 26th Amendment to the Constitution, which withdrew their recognition and privileges. (The US has had 27 amendments in over 200 years; India has already had 105 amendments since independence.)

From independence, the fortunes of Pakistan and India began to diverge. Pakistan remained a dominion of the British Empire until 1956, when it received a new constitution as an Islamic Republic, explicitly recognizing Allah's domination over the universe in its law. War with India in 1965 started an economic downturn, and the first democratic elections in 1970 didn't bring about democracy but instead led to the war with Bangladesh (East Pakistan) when the Awami League (a secular Bengali movement) won the elections in the east.

In 1971, President Yahya Khan launched Operation Searchlight. All political and student leaders in East Pakistan were arrested, and communications were cut off. He had assumed that opposition would crumble within a week. Genocide followed, with anywhere between 300,000 and three million Bangladeshis killed and ten million fleeing to India. In the end, it was India's intervention on the side of the independence fighters that brought about the independence of Bangladesh.

From 1972 to 1977, the Oxford-educated Zulfikar Ali Bhutto led the Pakistan People's Party to power on a socialist platform. He is an ambiguous figure, secular and internationalist, but also a violator of human rights (violently suppressing separatist movements) and a populist. He allied Pakistan with China, nationalized all industries, and carried out land reforms limiting the power of wealthy landowners. He also established the Pakistani nuclear weapons program. But he failed to create strong democratic institutions, and in 1977, he was deposed and imprisoned by the man he himself had put in charge of the army, Zia ul-Haq.

Pakistan saw over a decade of military rule, together with the growth of Islamic conservatism. After Zia's death in 1988, Benazir Bhutto, Zulfikar Ali Bhutto's daughter, was elected prime minister for the People's Party. The main opposition was Nawaz Sharif's center-right coalition, which eventually won power but was then deposed in a military coup by General Pervez Musharraf. After his resignation in 2008, Pakistan returned to democracy (though without Benazir Bhutto, who had been assassinated in 2007). However, the Taliban takeover of Afghanistan increased fundamentalist terrorism within the country, and the corruption of Nawaz Sharif (exposed in the Panama Papers) has destabilized the country. Following a no-confidence motion carried against former cricketer Imran Khan, Shehbaz Sharif, a wealthy businessman and brother of Nawaz Sharif, became Prime Minister.

Meanwhile, India saw more stability, with Congress ruling the country until 1977, gradually shifting from orthodox Socialism to a more mixed neo-liberal outlook under PM Manmohan Singh (2004-2014), who carried out economic liberalization and started a decade of high growth.

Nehru led India for thirteen years until his death in 1964, with Congress winning a landslide at every election. He invested in heavy industry, receiving investment from both the West and the Communist bloc enabled by his policy of non-alignment. Lal Bahadur Shastri, the next PM, kept most of Nehru's Cabinet and policies and made Nehru's daughter, Indira Gandhi, a minister; she succeeded him on his sudden death in 1966.

Indira Gandhi would dominate most of the next twenty years of Indian politics, filling the office of prime minister—apart from three years in opposition against the Janata Party—until her assassination in 1984. Her focus was on removing poverty, notably through the Green Revolution, enabling India to achieve its aim of food security. She also nationalized banks, insurance companies, and the cotton, steel, coal, and textile industries.

Indira Gandhi in 1989.
https://commons.wikimedia.org/wiki/File:Prime_Minister_Indira_Gandhi_in_the_US.jpg

Although Mrs. Gandhi introduced a State of Emergency from 1975 to 1977, during which she effectively ruled by decree, she remained true to her father's principles of democratic rule, calling elections in 1977, which she lost to the Janata Party. (In 1979, the Janata government started to fall apart, and Gandhi regained power in 1980.) She also made English the de facto official language, refusing to make Hindi compulsory, which gained her strong support in the south and showed a true pan-Indian vision.

However, this vision was not shared by the Sikh-led Akali Dal Party, which came to power in Punjab state. Militancy grew, using the area around the Golden Temple in Amritsar as a base, and in 1983, General Atwal of the Punjab Police was shot dead as he left the temple. In June 1984, Mrs. Gandhi ordered Operation Blue Star to clear the militants out of the temple compound. It achieved this objective but at the cost of the deaths of many innocent pilgrims and extensive damage to the temple. Later that year, two of her Sikh bodyguards assassinated her in retaliation.

Indira Gandhi was succeeded by her son, Rajiv Gandhi; he, in turn, was assassinated in 1991, and after a reversal in the party's fortunes, his widow Sonia (Italian by birth) took over as leader of Congress in 1998. She won the 2004 general elections and was chosen to lead the United Progressive Alliance but chose Manmohan Singh as prime minister instead of taking the post herself. He remained in the post until 2014 and was the first Sikh PM. He had already been the finance minister during the 1990s, deregulating the "License Raj" and reducing the state's control of the economy. The economy responded well to his intervention; under his premiership, GDP grew by as much as 9 percent a year.

Singh also introduced the National Rural Health Mission of 2005, bringing decentralized health care to rural areas with over half a million local health workers, and the Right to Education Act 2009, making education free and compulsory for all children ages 6 to 14.

More recently, Congress appears to have lost its electoral appeal; the Bharatiya Janata Party's Narendra Modi has been prime minister since 2014, leading a Hindu nationalist government to victory over a Congress that was seen as corrupt and out of touch. He relied greatly on his reputation as chief minister of Gujarat, seen as a minister who brought economic growth and infrastructure development to his state. However, his party has shifted away from secularism and become more authoritarian, though India's economy has continued to grow strongly.

One new party arrived in 2012 with the foundation of the Aam Aadmi or "Common Man" party by anti-corruption campaigner Arvind Kejriwal. The party won the city of Delhi elections—Kejriwal still serves as Chief Minister of Delhi—and it is now well represented in Punjab. It has also started to win seats in Gujarat and Goa but nationally hasn't yet made a huge impact.

Chapter 8: Indian Culture

Indian life today is a strange mixture of modernity and tradition. You can walk from a sagging stall made of plastic sacking and bamboo, selling onions wholesale, and within a minute be inside a bright, modern shopping mall full of mobile phone shops. You can be twenty minutes away from a tech campus where IBM and Microsoft have offices and see a sleeping cow in the middle of the street bring traffic to a stop. Or, you can take the air-conditioned Delhi metro to a ruined medieval fort where kids are playing cricket in the dirt.

But nonetheless, India's history has left its mark on Indian culture. For instance, the idea of renunciation is still strong; people still leave their jobs and normal lives to become monks, hermits, or ascetics. Most homes have a shrine room or at least a corner where a picture of a god or the Kaaba in Mecca is taped up on the wall. And you'll still be asked to take your shoes off while visiting a temple or a home.

Family Life, Education, and Sports

Marriages are still often arranged, and in the "marriage season" (November through February), you'll frequently see a traditional bridegroom's cavalcade, often accompanied by a slightly less traditional sound system. The urban middle classes are moving away from arranged marriages, and some newspapers give a discount on classified advertisements for those looking for a partner without making any caste distinctions. (However, you'll still often find ads looking for "light-skinned" partners; this is a real mark of status in India, and skin-lightening lotions still sell well to girls looking to improve their looks.)

But gaining the in-laws' approval is still crucial for brides since they'll often move into their husband's family home. Several generations often live together, and there's a real respect for elders, who receive the care they need from their children and grandchildren.

Indian women are still struggling with the patriarchy. Some Western gender differentiations don't exist; for instance, plenty of women become engineers, and you'll also find women in road-building gangs. While many high-profile rape cases have shown the huge tension of gender relations in India (particularly as many young men can't afford to marry), things are changing. Many professional families are now settling for two daughters instead of trying for a son. Colonial-era laws criminalizing homosexuality have also been successfully challenged in the Supreme Court, and hijras (male transsexuals) were recognized officially as a third gender in 2014.

Indians have great respect for education, and one of the remaining influences of the Raj is the school uniform still worn by many Indian pupils. It is not unusual to see graduation photos even in the poorest households, as frequently parents will live frugally to ensure a good education for their children, both male and female. However, educational standards vary widely across the country. While there is almost universal literacy in Kerala, Bihar, Arunachal Pradesh, and Rajasthan still only manage 67-69 percent, and female literacy is only just over 50 percent.

Indian dress is varied. Middle-class workers will often wear Western business attire, but women will often still wear saris or a salwar suit (tunic and leggings with a matching scarf or wrap). In rural areas, local and tribal dress is often common. Muslim men may wear Western clothes or a kurta (long white shirt) with trousers.

However, religious rites sometimes have particular requirements. Some temples require men to wear a dhoti (a loincloth such as Gandhi wore), and some will not admit men who are wearing clothing on their torsos—they must be bare-chested.

India has been able to enjoy its revenge on Britain by adopting the sport of cricket and frequently beating the English at their own game. Indian children will play anywhere they can find a flat bit of ground and a stick and stone to use as a bat and ball. The Indian Premier League is now the best-attended cricket league in the world and a multi-million-dollar business; it's even broadcast live on YouTube.

Second only to cricket comes kabaddi, a traditional sport something like a game of tag in which a "raider" from one team aims to tag as many of the other team's seven members as possible without being tackled. So far, India has won every single Kabaddi World Cup, with Iran as runners-up each time.

Indian Arts

India has a rich artistic heritage. From the rock-cut temples of Ellora and Mamallapuram to the perfection of the Taj Mahal, its architecture is fascinating; even the British Raj couldn't resist Indian styles, creating what's known as the Indo-Saracenic school for public buildings such as Mumbai's CST railway terminal, the Taj Mahal hotel, and the Howrah railway station in Kolkata.

Images of the gods are often found in Indian art, both as cult statues (murti) and as figures in narrative or miniature paintings. For instance, the palace in Bundi, Rajasthan, contains rooms covered with paintings of the life of Krishna; that's also a favorite subject for Rajput miniature painters. While the Mughal court was Muslim, ruling out portrayals of deities, the painting of portraits and historical narratives was encouraged. Portraits were often highly observant and individual, including those of Hindu holy men as well as emperors and their retainers.

More recently, India has seen a rediscovery of village and tribal art traditions, such as Madhubani painting. Originally used to decorate the walls of houses, this painting has now been adapted to use on paper. Strong black ink patterns surround vivid colors, with traditional motifs such as fish, the tree of life, and the stories of Krishna and Radha.

India also has a rich tradition of decorative arts, including jewelry and textiles. Many of these are very local, such as Bandhani tie-and-dye in Gujarat and Phulkari geometrical embroidery from Punjab. Varanasi still has a silk-weaving industry, as does Chanderi, where the local prince set up a mixed cotton and silk weaving workshop to provide employment.

While some artists restrict themselves to producing traditional-style works for the tourist trade, fine contemporary art is being created, too. M. F. Husain created intensely-colored, cubist-influenced art, taking topics as diverse as folklore, religious tales, Mother Teresa, and the Raj. Though a Muslim by birth, he painted Hindu gods, too—eventually self-exiling after his naked Mother India painting got him embroiled in a culture war with Hindu right-wingers.

Prominent on the world art scene is Anish Kapoor, an artist of mixed Bombay Jewish and Hindu heritage who is now a dual British-Indian national. Kapoor's explorations of matter and void have often drawn on Hindu symbolism. For instance, he uses holes bored in stone and filled with vivid pigments to create forms that evoke Hindu shrines and the sacred color red (for instance, the red wax in his Svayambh, which evokes blood, sacrifice, or transfiguration).

Indian music has gained many admirers in the west; sitar player Ravi Shankar played with both violinist Yehudi Menuhin and composer Philip Glass, and George Harrison of the Beatles was profoundly influenced by Shankar's playing, too. Classical Indian music is based on the idea of tala, a cyclical rhythmic structure joined with raga, a melodic framework. The raga is not just a scale, as in Western music, but includes certain motifs and evokes specific feelings. There are morning, evening, and night ragas; while some are serious and sad, others are lighthearted or joyous.

Bhajans are frequently sung in temples, and Indian Muslims have developed a similar tradition of sacred singing called Qawwali, of which the Pakistani singer Nusrat Fateh Ali Khan was the best-known performer.

In modern India, though, it's not classical or religious singers who are the best known, but "playback singers" who sing the musical numbers for actors in Bollywood films. While they may not appear on the screen, they are still celebrated, sometimes giving concerts on their own account. Asha Bhosle and Lata Mangeshkar were the two most celebrated playback singers.

Indian film has seen some major art film auteurs, such as Satyajit Ray, but its best-known product is Bollywood (a portmanteau word made from Bombay + Hollywood). Bollywood movies generally feature a lot of song and dance routines, a love interest, and a stereotyped mustache-twirling villain. Actors such as Amitabh Bachchan (who has also worked as a playback singer) are among the richest and best-known celebrities in India. (Bachchan was also a Congress MP for Allahabad for a term, gaining a commanding majority at the election.)

India also counts not just one but two "Tollywoods"—Telegu cinema in the south and the Bengali film industry based in Tollygunge, Kolkata— as well as a thriving Tamil language cinema based in Chennai. The latter created perhaps one of the oddest movies ever filmed, Guruvayur

Keshavan (1977), the biography of a famed temple elephant. (Amitabh Bachchan's stint in politics was a one-off. But the 1960s film actress Jayaram Jayalalithaa became chief minister of Tamil Nadu, racking up six terms in office.)

Food and Festivals

"Indian food is spicy," people say. And that's true, but the kind of spice and the method of cooking varies from one part of the subcontinent to another.

For instance, Gujarati food is usually vegetarian and quite sweet, with the addition of a little jaggery (palm sugar) to most dishes. In Bengal, mustard is at the heart of most dishes, together with green chili; meat is commonly eaten, often marinated in yogurt and spice before cooking. Goan cuisine mixes Portuguese and Indian influences, with vinegar to give extra piquancy to meat dishes and the frequent use of pork.

While for many families, rice and dal (lentils) is a standard dish, Indian cooking can be very luxurious. For instance, the cooking of the Mughal court left its traces on the Lucknow tradition, with kebabs, meat stews, fluffy breads, and long-stewed chicken dishes with a fine blend of spices. On the opposite end of the spectrum, Indian street food includes the panipuri, a puffed-up pastry ball full of tangy beans and potatoes—or wickedly full of hot chili sauce—and bhel puri, puffed rice with tamarind chutney, fried vermicelli ("Bombay mix"), chopped onions and tomatoes, and coriander leaf.

Indian festivals are always overwhelming events. Holi celebrates the arrival of spring, and it's the festival of colors, quite literally, in which you're liable to be sprayed with bright-colored dye or powder. Most people "play Holi" with their friends and family and give no quarter. Diwali, the festival of lights, is at the other end of the year, in early autumn; it includes fireworks, gift-giving, and a lot of confectionery.

Many localities have their own festivals. The Shia Muslim rite of Muharram is celebrated in Lucknow with processions of portable shrines known as tazias, while in Kolkata, Durga Puja worships the demon-killing goddess Durga with portable shrines set up to the goddess around the city. (At the end of the festival, they're taken in procession to the river and immersed.)

Christmas is also celebrated, notably by the Christian communities of Kerala and Tamil Nadu, which hang lighted paper stars outside their houses.

One thing that belongs with every Indian festival is noise. Fireworks are a favorite, but you'll hear brass bands, drumming, and chanting, as well as amplified music. In fact, noise is a facet of Indian life that's ever-present. The Indian Highway Code doesn't actually contain a rule that motorists must blow their horns every five seconds, but it certainly sounds like it!

Chapter 9: Influential Indians in History

History is full of influential and incredible Indians. Akbar, for instance, is an amazing character: an illiterate man who supported scholarship, a Turkic Muslim who threw his court open to every race and religion, and an extreme sports fan who rode in elephant fights for fun. This chapter will look at a few influential Indians you may not have heard of.

Mother Teresa was a different kind of amazing. In fact, she wasn't Indian by birth; she was Albanian (though she adopted Indian citizenship). She spent her novitiate in Darjeeling and taught at Loreto Convent in Kolkata until she felt the call to do something more. Leaving her order, she founded the Missionaries of Charity in 1946. She adapted the Indian sari as the dress of the order, which ran soup kitchens, homes for lepers, and hospices for those dying of tuberculosis and, later, of AIDS. The order also managed children's clinics, schools, and orphanages.

Not all Indians approve of Mother Teresa. Some feel she motivated what has been called "poverty porn," a view of India as a backward and uncaring society; others believe she imposed Christian values that were inappropriate in a Hindu culture and secular nation. However, the Catholic Church is in no doubt about her contribution: she was canonized in 2016.

A very different kind of hero was the Indian revolutionary Bhagat Singh. He was part of a growing militant movement in the 1930s, often writing for Urdu and Punjabi newspapers and for the journal of the Workers and Peasants Party. He was a prominent member of the Hindustan Republican Association (HRA). When Lala Lajpat Rai, a prominent member of Congress and of the independence movement, was killed in a police baton charge against protesters in Lahore, the HRA vowed to avenge his death.

Singh conspired with several others to kill the Punjab superintendent of police, James Scott. Unfortunately, he mistook the target and killed a lower-ranking officer, John Saunders. Despite a police chase and a massive search operation, all the conspirators escaped Lahore. Singh cut off his hair (grown long, in Sikh style, though he was an atheist) and swapped his turban for a felt hat.

Singh later participated in the bombing of the Delhi Assembly and—with his accomplice Batukeshwar Dutt—was arrested, tried, and sentenced to life in prison. Later, the police discovered two bomb factories that had been set up by the HRA and arrested several members of the party. They realized that Singh was involved not only in the Delhi bombing but also in the murder of Saunders. Two of his accomplices in the murder plan informed on him, making the case against him watertight.

While awaiting trial, Singh led a hunger strike of Indian prisoners who claimed that they should be treated as political prisoners. Both Nehru and Jinnah showed themselves sympathetic to Singh's cause. He was so weak that, when he came to trial, he had to be carried into the courtroom on a stretcher.

Singh received the death sentence along with two of his companions despite many appeals for clemency. He remains an iconic figure for many Indians. The Indian Post Office even devoted a stamp to him in 1968, wearing his trademark hat.

Guru Nanak was the founder of the Sikh religion and the first of its ten gurus (nine of whom were human beings). The Granth Sahib, the collected scriptures, is considered the tenth guru. He was a great traveler, though some of the stories of his travels may have been exaggerated later. He made it as far as Ladakh, in the Himalayas, where he left a walking stick pushed into the ground; it is now a venerable tree, the Datun Sahib.

His teaching of one god (Ik Onkar) reflects both the monotheism of Islam and the bhakti movement's idea that everyone can have a direct experience of God without rituals or priests. There is a rather lovely story that, when he died, the Hindus and Muslims both wanted to claim his body as a relic. But, when they pulled on the sheet in which he had been shrouded, it turned out to be filled with fresh flowers.

His ideas are expressed very simply: "Vand shhako, kirat karo, naam japo," which means share, work honestly, and say God's name. Whichever gurdwara (Sikh temple) you visit and whatever your beliefs, you will be welcome to share the communal meal (langur)—a practical example of Sikh "sharing" and social service.

B.R. Ambedkar was one of the founding fathers of the Indian Republic often overlooked by the history books. Unlike most of the other men involved in the independence movement, Ambedkar was not primarily a lawyer but an economist who was educated at Columbia and the London School of Economics. (He did have legal qualifications, too.)

He was born into the Dalit (Untouchable) caste and was the first of his caste to go to Elphinstone College in Mumbai. He was chairman of the drafting committee for the Indian Constitution and ensured it was progressive—including civil liberties, rights for women, and the reservation of jobs for scheduled castes and tribes, the equivalent of affirmative action. He also argued for a separate Dalit electorate, putting him at odds with Gandhi.

B.R. Ambedkar.
https://commons.wikimedia.org/wiki/File:Dr._Bhimrao_Ambedkar.jpg

Ambedkar led satyagraha movements to gain rights for Dalits. In Mahad, he fought for the Dalits' right to draw water from the communal water tank and, at Kalaram Temple in Nashik, to allow Dalits into the temple. Throughout his career, he suffered prejudice because of his caste. At school, he was not allowed to touch the water jug, and when he became a professor in Mumbai, his students would not share drinking water with him. His crusade was a deeply personal one.

Eventually, he converted to Buddhism alongside nearly half a million of his followers. His form of Buddhism, called Navayana, is a politically-engaged form of Buddhism THAT rejects metaphysics and mysticism in favor of the pursuit of social justice.

Women are often left out of Indian history, partly since women of the higher class among both Rajputs and Mughals lived in privacy. Wives of the Mughal emperor were often referred to by honorific court names or by their place of birth, and it was a form of praise to say that no one knew their real names. However, women have very often refused to conform to these expectations.

Velu Nachiyar (1730-1796) was a princess of Ramanathapuram who, as an only daughter, was brought up trained in combat and archery, as well as book learning. She married the king of Sivaganga, but in 1780, he was killed in a battle with the East India Company.

Velu went to Haidar Ali of Mysore, asking him for help, and obtained 5,000 soldiers as well as some heavy artillery. She devoted herself to campaigning against the Company—the first Indian queen to do so—and successfully regained her kingdom, ruling it for ten years before abdicating in favor of her daughter Vellachi. She is known as "Veeramangai," the brave woman, to Tamils.

Another famous freedom fighter was Rani Lakshmibai of Jhansi. She had married the Maharaja of Jhansi, Gangadar Rao Newalkar, in 1842, but their only son died, leaving the maharaja without an heir. They decided to adopt a boy called Anand Rao, the son of a cousin, and renamed him Damodar Rao. But on the death of the maharaja in 1853, the British applied the Doctrine of Lapse and claimed Jhansi. Lakshmibai stayed put, and for the time being, it seems the British were willing to let the matter lie.

Lakshmibai rode well and shot well; she also fenced, lifted weights, and wrestled. But she doesn't appear to have been a political mastermind—at least, it is difficult to be certain what side she was on. In

1857, when the Indian Rebellion in Meerut began, she asked the British for permission to raise forces for her own protection. However, the fort was seized by rebel Bengal infantry, who massacred the British garrison in Jhansi and extorted money from her.

She assumed command of Jhansi, but the forces of Orchha and Datia states, allied to the East India Company, decided to invade. Many of the British believed she had abetted the massacre of the British forces, so when she appealed to them for help, she got no answer. She managed to defeat the invaders on her own, and when the British turned up some time later and demanded her surrender, she defended the city bravely but unsuccessfully.

The British were already in the city when she mounted her horse Badal with her son Damodar Rao on her back and jumped from the ramparts of the fort. The horse died, but she escaped with her son, first to Kalpi and then to Gwalior. There, she fought as a sowar (cavalry officer) and was killed in the battle for the city.

Mirabai was also a princess, but her life was very different from the Rani of Jhansi's. She was born into a Rajput royal family in the sixteenth century, but little more than that is known for certain of her early life. She became a devotee of Krishna and is widely regarded as one of the great bhakti poets. Her poems address him as "the dark one" and sometimes "the mountain lifter," referring to the story that he picked up Mount Govardhan to use as an umbrella. The poems clearly show her personal devotion, representing her as Krishna's lover and servant, completely surrendered to him.

Mirabai has also become a potent symbol of feminine freedom—a woman who refused her heritage and stuck to her beliefs despite all opposition from her family. Her bhajans are still sung today.

Sarojini Naidu was another lyric poet, writing in both Persian and English and known to her contemporaries as "the Nightingale of India." But she was also one of Gandhi's colleagues, a fervent nationalist, and the only woman on the Congress Working Committee.

Naidu was educated in England, where she became a suffragette. She had a luxurious lifestyle, refusing to sit on the floor when she visited Gandhi, wear simple clothes, or eat his "disgusting" food, and yet she happily went to jail for her principles. She had to fight Gandhi for the right to go on the Salt March—he thought it would be too tough for women—but after his arrest, Gandhi told her to take over from him as leader of the campaign.

Following independence, Naidu was appointed governor of Uttar Pradesh, the first woman to fill this office.

Gulbadan was the daughter of the Mughal emperor Babur, sister of Humayun, and much-loved aunt of Akbar. When she was 65, Akbar asked her to write an account of Humayun's life, and it is through her writings that we know the world of the royal Mughal women. She describes Hamida Banu Begum, Akbar's mother and a huge influence on the emperor; she records the way women reacted to the world around them and the way the harem exerted influence on diplomatic affairs. Her book is a counterpart to Abu'l-Fazl's account of Akbar's reign; it shows a mirror image of the male court, one that is made up of women.

Gulbadan seems to have been a strong character. She decided to make the pilgrimage to Mecca and led a woman-only hajj which took her seven years. She stayed in Mecca for four years and was shipwrecked on the Yemeni coast on her way back. When she died at the age of eighty, Akbar grieved for her as he seems to have done for no one other than his father.

Mary Kom would probably love the Rani of Jhansi and Velu Nachiyar if they were able to meet up. Mangte Chungneijang Mary Kom, to give her full name, was born in a poor Christian tribal family in the state of Manipur in northeast India. She started as a keen athlete, running and throwing javelin, but decided to take up boxing when she was 15, keeping it secret from her father. He didn't find out until she won the state boxing championship.

Her titles include six gold medals in the World Amateur Boxing Championships and a bronze medal in the 2012 Olympics. She's also the mother of three sons, and in 2018, she and her husband adopted a daughter and found time to sit in the Rajya Sabha (Senate) for six years.

Chapter 10: Buddhism vs Hinduism

India is the cradle of three faiths: Hinduism, Buddhism, and Jainism. But their three fates were very different. Hinduism, though exported to Southeast Asia early on, is now the main religion only in India (and, in a rather different form, in Bali). Buddhism made its way to Sri Lanka, Southeast Asia, and China, and through China to Korea and Japan; another form of Buddhism made its way to Tibet and Mongolia, but the faith practically died out in India after the medieval era.

The Jain religion, on the other hand, remained in India. But, unlike Buddhism, it did not proselytize actively outside the subcontinent. Today, there is a large Jain community in the states of Maharashtra, Rajasthan, Karnataka, and Gujarat, particularly in Mumbai, but overall, it is a small minority making up less than half a percent of the total population. It is, by the way, the minority with the highest rate of literacy by far and a wealthy community involved in commerce and finance.

Hinduism is a religion that is quite literally rooted in the landscape of India, from the sites of Krishna's childhood around Vrindavan and Mathura or his kingdom in Dwarka to individual sacred stones and trees. The rivers, in particular, are considered sacred; many temples have sculptures of the Ganges and Yamuna personified as goddesses guarding the door to the inner sanctuary.

Sometimes, the sacred landscape is recreated. For instance, at Mount Abu, at the foot of the Gangotri Glacier in the Himalayas, there is a holy spring called Gaumukh that is channeled into a tank through a cow's head spout; it is considered the source of the Ganges. The most widespread example of this is the way temples evoke Mount Meru in the Himalayas, Shiva's home, and the center of the universe, both through the spire of the temple representing the mountain and the windowless interior garbhagriha sanctuary representing the cave in which he practiced his austerities.

Buddhism doesn't have this kind of attachment to the landscape, though the sites of Buddha's birth, enlightenment, first sermon, and death are now pilgrimage sites attracting visitors from all over the Buddhist world. Perhaps this freed the religion to expand to other countries in a way that Hinduism found more difficult. (Even now, orthodox Hindus consider leaving India an impurity. A monk who had traveled to the US and Europe found that conservative priests wanted to ban him from becoming the head of a temple. Gandhi was excommunicated by the Bania caste when he went to London to study law and remained an out-caste for the rest of his life.)

Right from the beginning, Hindu thinkers appear to have been concerned with the question of where things came from, with the existence of emptiness and void. The Rig Veda asks questions about creation rather than telling a creation myth:

1. THEN was not non-existent nor existent: there was no realm of air, no sky beyond it.

   What covered in, and where? and what gave shelter? Was water there, unfathomed depth of water?

2. Death was not then, nor was there aught immortal: no sign was there, the day's and night's divider.

   That One Thing, breathless, breathed by its own nature: apart from it was nothing whatsoever.

3. Darkness there was: at first concealed in darkness this All was indiscriminate chaos.

   All that existed then was void and form less: by the great power of Warmth was born that Unit.

4. Thereafter rose Desire in the beginning, Desire, the primal seed and germ of Spirit.

   Sages who searched with their heart's thought discovered the existent's kinship in the non-existent.

5. Transversely was their severing line extended: what was above it then, and what below it?

There were begetters, there were mighty forces, free action here and energy up yonder

6. Who verily knows and who can here declare it, whence it was born and whence comes this creation?

The Gods are later than this world's production. Who knows then whence it first came into being?

7. He, the first origin of this creation, whether he formed it all or did not form it, Whose eye controls this world in highest heaven, he verily knows it, or perhaps he knows not.

(Rig Veda 10.129)

This concern with the nature of reality gives rise to the idea of cycles of time in which the universe is created and destroyed over and over. The idea of Brahma, Shiva, and Vishnu as a kind of "trinity" of gods is most likely a Victorian interpolation, but the dynamic of creation, preservation, and destruction is authentically Hindu.

Buddhism, too, has this dizzying idea of a void at the center of things. The world is made up of illusions; human life is an illusion. Nirvana, like the Hindu moksha, is a salvation that is represented as release from the multiplicity and illusive nature of the physical world. The cycle of times, too, finds its place in Buddhism, with the concept of different universes and different eras.

The ideas of reincarnation and karma are found in both religions, stemming from the idea of cyclicality. Karma is seen as a natural law, the way things work; each action brings about its consequences. However, there is no idea of reward or punishment associated with it, as there is with Christian or Muslim ideas of heaven and hell; karma is simply the way things balance.

Spiritual practices are also in many ways common between Buddhism and Hinduism. Both religions use forms of yoga and meditation to liberate the soul from distraction by the illusory world; both use mantras, sacred chants, as a part of ritual and meditation. Om, or Aum, the sacred seed-syllable, is seen as the vibration from which the world arises; it invokes the single reality behind the illusory world of appearances. Common mantras include the name of a god: Om Namah Shivaya, honoring Shiva, or Hare Krishna Hare Rama. In Buddhism, one of the earliest mantras is Namo Buddhaya, "homage to the Buddha."

Although some authorities attempt to define Hinduism as polytheistic and Buddhism as monotheistic, once you start looking in detail at the philosophies involved, there is a certain fluidity about both Hinduism and Buddhism. For instance, many Shaivites will tell you that they believe all gods are one; Mahayana Buddhists, one of the two different schools that evolved over the centuries, have many different Buddhas and bodhisattvas but will tell you that these, too, are only illusions made to bring you closer to the truth.

This fluidity is built into the idea of Brahman and Atman, the world soul and the individual soul. The individual soul can commune and even fuse with the world soul, becoming absorbed in it. In bhakti, devotees achieve complete immersion in their god: some sources tell of Mirabai being absorbed physically into a statue of Lord Krishna.

Men and gods overlap. Vishnu has several incarnations, or avatars, including Krishna, Rama, and the Buddha. At the Mahabodhi Temple in Bodh Gaya, the site of Buddha's enlightenment, most of the pilgrims are Buddhists, but there are always a few Hindu holy men with long white beards and hair and bright yellow robes, worshiping Vishnu in the avatar of Buddha. In Tibetan Buddhism, on the other hand, some Hindu gods find themselves transformed into Buddhist deities, such as Ganesh, who becomes Ganapati, and the jolly little god of wealth, Jambhala—but they are only subsidiary figures, subservient to the Buddhas.

This kind of fluidity is also typical of Indian art and architecture. For instance, many temples are made up of repeated motifs which turn out to be practically miniature temples. In Mughal times, a particularly delightful artistic endeavor was making up elephants or swans out of other animals or human bodies—which is real, the elephant or the human figures? There's no easy answer.

India has had a literate culture since the first millennium. Inscriptions are everywhere: there are written land grants, the Ashoka pillars, mantras, and Persian calligraphy. But unlike Judeo-Christian religions, neither Hinduism nor Buddhism has a single sacred text—they have a corpus of texts of differing authority. For instance, a Krishna devotee might read the Bhagavad Gita as their only guide, going deeper and deeper into its meanings as they re-read it again and again, even though it's just a small part of the larger Mahabharata.

In Buddhism, too, there is no one text that stands above all. Buddhism has a concept of skillful means (upaya), that is, the way that the Buddha's message can be tailored for each individual to help them towards enlightenment. That might be the Tripitaka (Buddha's teachings as written down by those who heard him or received them through the oral tradition), but it might include the Jataka tales of Buddha's earlier lives or the Tantric texts that emerged later. In one sermon, Buddha simply held up a flower, and his student Mahakasyapa became enlightened simply by seeing it.

Why did Buddhism leave India while Hinduism remained strong? After the end of the Gupta Empire, Buddhism seems to have lost most of its patronage from royal sources. Perhaps one of the reasons is that Hinduism changed, with devotional movements offering individuals a more meaningful and personal relationship with the gods. The Buddhists and Jains had challenged ritual Hinduism and the caste system; bhakti, which did not allow caste to come between the worshiper and their god, made up for what had been missing in Hinduism.

Another possible reason is that Buddhism became a monastic religion, and the large Buddhist monasteries became divorced from day-to-day life; Buddhism didn't offer much advice for lay people. (This is something the Jains certainly did offer, with a huge amount of advice on how to live well in an ordinary family.) On the other hand, Hinduism offered a range of different ways for the individual to be involved in religion, whether through rites of puja, singing bhajans, making pilgrimages, or living the life of a renunciate yogi.

At the same time, when the Turks invaded through Afghanistan, the fact that Buddhism had spread to other countries made it easier for monks to migrate to the Himalayas, China, Sri Lanka, and Southeast Asia. Once Buddhist monasteries had been sacked, the Sangha died out as its leaders fled. Since most of the large Buddhist centers were in northern India, they experienced the brunt of early invasions. Hindus, on the contrary, were well represented in southern India, which could resist invasion.

It is also worth considering that Buddhism did not need India in the same way that Hinduism did. It did not rely on a sacred landscape, and its more thorough-going dismissal of the world as illusory meant it was not tied to sacred sites in the same way as Hinduism. On the other hand, Hindu movements such as bhakti intensified the presence of Hinduism in the landscape, for instance with Chaitanya's rediscovery of the land of Braj and the landscape of Krishna's birth and early life around Vrindavan and Mathura.

Conclusion

The Republic of India is now three-quarters of a century old. India itself is several millennia older.

But the Republic still has some unfinished business. There are still hard feelings about colonialism, which came to the fore recently with the accession of King Charles III. Indians fretted about whether the queen consort would wear a crown including the famous Koh-i-Noor diamond that once belonged to the Sikh Empire—and possibly, before that, to Shah Jahan as part of his Peacock Throne. (She won't.)

There are also still hard feelings about partition. Pakistan and India have had four wars and numerous skirmishes and are still in conflict. Bangladesh, on the other hand, has begun to establish a positive relationship with India. However, Narendra Modi's espousal of Hindutva and anti-Muslim rhetoric make it hard to see India becoming fully reconciled with its Muslim neighbors.

It's still a challenge to bring poorer states like Bihar and Rajasthan up to the status of wealthier states like Gujarat and Kerala. Literacy rates, economic production, and wealth vary very greatly between states, hence the presence of many migrant workers from poorer states in Delhi and other big cities.

But India is definitely reaching for the future. Young Indians are often fearsomely well-educated, particularly in scientific and technological subjects; India has a huge high-tech economy. Everyone is on WhatsApp and Facebook, even in small villages, and India has now become the world's fastest-growing mobile payments market. Because English is widely spoken, the country has become home to numerous call centers, technical support centers, and software outsourcing businesses.

Economically, India has been shadowed by China. But a lot of China's recent progress has been driven by high indebtedness, and Chinese companies are not noted for their quality. Besides, Chinese businesses are controlled by the state. In India, on the other hand, anyone can set up a business; the cost of entry is low, and deregulation has removed many of the License Raj's roadblocks. The future is full of opportunity.

India's future? The Indian School of Business campus in Mohali.
MBAaspire11, CC BY-SA 3.0 <https://creativecommons.org/licenses/by-sa/3.0>, via Wikimedia Commons. https://en.wikipedia.org/wiki/File:ISB%27s_Mohali_Campus.jpg

Yet India retains its distinctive culture in a modern world. For instance, traditional Ayurvedic medicine is now researched in a scientific way and taught as an option in medical schools to students who have already learned Western sciences and anatomy. Tea stands and falooda parlous still outnumber McDonald's. And depending on the city, you may still be woken in the early morning by the muezzin or the sound of loudspeakers broadcasting "Om Nama Shivaya" from the local temple.

India might become the "silicon subcontinent." It might take the world of renewable energy by storm. But whatever happens, it's never going to be quite like anywhere else.

Dates

2600-1700 BCE	Harappan civilization
1500-500 BCE	Compilation of the Vedas
6th century BCE	Early states in Indo-Gangetic Plain: Mahavira, Buddha
327-5 BCE	Alexander the Great in India
321 BCE	Chandragupta founds the Mauryan dynasty
268 BCE	Ashoka accedes to the throne
185 BCE	End of Mauryan rule
180-65 BCE	Rule of Menander: Indo-Greek dynasty in NW
1st century CE	Kushan state founded
320	Accession of Chandragupta, founder of Gupta dynasty
410	Visit of Fa Hsien, "Monkey"

c. 550	Chalukya dynasty begins, Badami
c. 570	Pallava rule in Kanchi
712	Arab conquest of Sind
752	Rashtrakutas beat Chalukyas
770	Pala dynasty, eastern India
c. 900	Chola become powerful, South India
973	Chalukyas defeat Rashtrakutas
1075	Ramanuja
1110	Rise of the Hoysala dynasty
1192	Battle of Tarain, Muhammad Ghuri defeats Chauhan
1206	Establishment of Delhi sultanate
1279	End of Chola power
1398	Timur sacks Delhi
1526	First Battle of Panipat, at which Babur defeats the Lodi sultanate of Delhi
1540	Sher Shah Suri establishes the Sur Empire after conquering Humayun
1555	Humayun reconquers Hindustan
1556	Accession of Akbar: Second battle of Panipat, Mughals defeat Afghans
1562	Akbar abolishes jizya tax on non-Muslims
1572	Akbar takes Ahmedabad, Gujarat

1574	Akbar takes Patna
1600	Foundation of East India Company
1739	Persians sack Delhi
1751	Robert Clive seizes Arcot
1757	British defeat Siraj ud-Daulah in Bengal
1784	India Act brings the EIC under government control.
1799	Tipu Sultan of Mysore killed in battle, British take Seringapatam
1843	British capture Sind: doctrine of lapse
1853	Railway built from Thane to Bombay—first in India
1857	Sepoy Mutiny/First War of Independence
1876	Queen Victoria proclaimed Empress of India
1911	Delhi becomes capital
1919	Jallianwala Bagh massacre, Amritsar
1930	The Salt March
1947	Independence, Partition of India
1975	Sikkim incorporated into India

Glossary

Ahimsa - nonviolence, a central tenet of Buddhist and Jain faiths.

Ashram - a hermitage or religious community.

Bhajan - a devotional song (Hindu).

Bhakti - a movement which espouses gaining salvation through intense personal devotion to a god.

Bharat - India (as in Mahabharata).

Chaitya - Buddhist place of worship.

Chakravartin – "world-ruler," the ideal universal ruler; applied to rulers whose empire includes previously separate kingdoms, or is of great extent (e.g., Ashoka).

Darshan – "viewing" of an idol, a religious experience which bestows blessings on the worshiper.

Dhoti - loincloth.

Factory - in its original sense, a trading post through which a foreign power was able to channel its trade with India.

Gana-sangha - rule by tribal assembly, in which a king (raja) governed with the assistance of the assembly.

Gopura - a tower gateway (Southern India).

Hajj - the Muslim pilgrimage to Mecca.

Hindutva - an ideology which sees India as essentially (and potentially, exclusively) Hindu, espoused by the right wing and by the BJP Party.

Jagir - a district whose tax revenues were assigned to a holder, the jagirdar, under Mughal administration.

Jauhar - self-immolation when it was obvious that a fort was going to be taken. The women would usually burn themselves and the men would go on a suicidal sortie against the enemy.

Jizya - special tax on non-Muslims.

Mandapa - a pillared hall for public rituals, often attached to the sanctuary of a temple but sometimes separate.

Mandir - a temple.

Mansab - a military pay grade in the Mughal empire, held by a mansabdar.

Matha or mutt - a Hindu monastery.

Moksha - salvation (for Hindus): a similar concept to Buddhist nirvana.

Puja - worshiping a deity by giving it food, incense, etc.

Qawwali - a form of Muslim devotional song.

Raga - a basic musical mode, including a scale and certain melodic motifs.

Raj – "rule"; British Raj, the period of direct British rule of India from 1858 to 1947.

Raja, maharaja - ruler, great ruler: title of Indian kings.

Sallekhana - the Jain vow of fasting to the death; gradual reduction of food intake.

Sangha - community; specifically, the Buddhist monastic community.

Sari or saree - form of dress for Indian women consisting of a single draped piece of cloth.

Sati or suttee - immolation of a widow on the funeral pyre of her dead husband: now criminalized.

Satyagraha - non-violent protest or civil disobedience.

Sepoy - an Indian soldier.

Shaivite - any sect or person devoted to the God Shiva.

Shikara - spire of a northern style Indian temple.

Sowar - an Indian horseback warrior.

Stupa - a mound erected to enclose Buddhist relics.

Swadeshi – "made in India"; the movement to boycott British imports and use only Indian materials and products.

Swaraj - independence.

Vaishnavite - person or sect devoted to the God Vishnu.

Vihara - a Buddhist monastery.

Vimana - spire of a southern style Indian temple.

Zamindar - a landowner who leases his land to tenant farmers.

Here's another book by Enthralling History that you might like

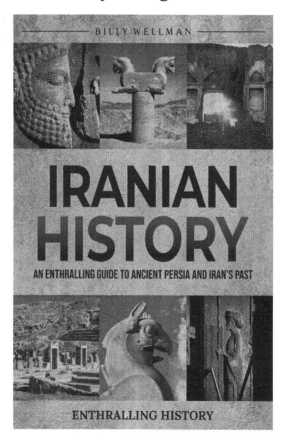

Free limited time bonus

Stop for a moment. We have a free bonus set up for you. The problem is this: we forget 90% of everything that we read after 7 days. Crazy fact, right? Here's the solution: we've created a printable, 1-page pdf summary for this book that you're reading now. All you have to do to get your free pdf summary is to go to the following website:

https://livetolearn.lpages.co/enthrallinghistory/

Once you do, it will be intuitive. Enjoy, and thank you!

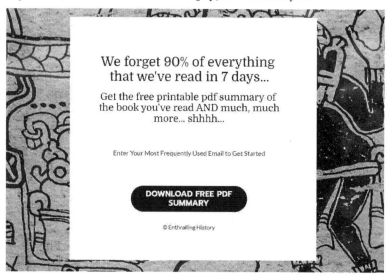

We forget 90% of everything
that we've read in 7 days...

Get the free printable pdf summary of
the book you've read AND much, much
more... shhhh...

Enter Your Most Frequently Used Email to Get Started

**DOWNLOAD FREE PDF
SUMMARY**

© Enthralling History

Bibliography

Anon. Rig Veda. Translated Griffith, Ralph TH. 1896.

Babur: tr. Annette Susannah Beveridge. Baburnama, a memoir. 2017 (reprint).

Bharne V & Kruske B. Rediscovering the Hindu Temple. Cambridge Scholars Publishing. 2012.

Chakravarty, Sudeep. Plassey: The Battle That Changed the Course of Indian History. 2020.

Collins, Larry & Lapierre, Dominique. Freedom at Midnight. 1975.

Dalrymple, William. White Mughals. Penguin. 2002.

– Nine Lives. In Search of the Sacred in Modern India. Bloomsbury. 2009.

– The Anarchy: The Relentless Rise of the East India Company. Bloomsbury. 2019.

Eck, Diana. India, a Sacred Geography. 2011.

Eraly, Abraham. The Mughal World. 2007.

Gandhi, Mahatma. Third Class in Indian Railways. 1917.

Godden, Rumer. Gulbadan: Portrait of a Rose Princess at the Mughal Court. 1980.

Herman, Arthur. Gandhi and Churchill: The Epic Rivalry That Destroyed an Empire and Forged Our Age. Random House Digital. 2008.

Michell, George: The Hindu Temple. University of Chicago Press. 1988.

Mukhoty, Ira. Akbar the Great Mughal: A Definitive Biography. 2020.

Nossov, Konstantin. Indian Castles 1206-1526.

Preston, Diana and Michael: A Teardrop on the Cheek of Time. Doubleday. 2007.

Smith, Vincent. Ashoka: The Buddhist Emperor of India. Clarendon Press, Oxford, 1920.

Thapar, Romila. The Penguin History of Early India from the Origins to AD 1300. London 2002.

Tharoor, Shashi. India: From Midnight to the Millennium. 1997.

--- Inglorious Empire: What the British Did to India. 2016.

--- Why I Am a Hindu. 2018.

--- Ambedkar: A life. 2022.

Video

"Sarmada Foundation: Madhubani, a sacred tradition"

https://www.youtube.com/watch?v=XO7KPnENbf4&list=WL&index=201&t=1s

Printed in Great Britain
by Amazon

50250070R00059

Journey
of the
Spirit

———

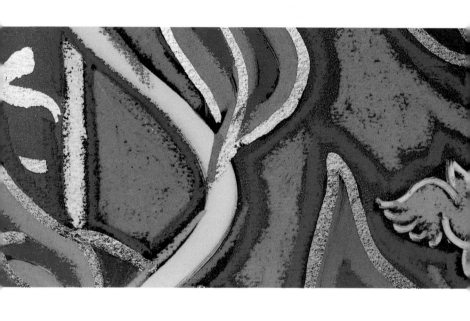

The Heart of Christianity Explored

JOURNEY
of the
SPIRIT

Mary Batchelor

LION
Giftlines

For Pauline, Graham and Oliver

Published by
Lion Publishing plc
Sandy Lane West, Oxford, England
ISBN 0 7459 3392 0
Albatross Books Pty Ltd
PO Box 320, Sutherland, NSW 2232, Australia
ISBN 0 7324 1374 5

First edition 1997
10 9 8 7 6 5 4 3 2 1 0

A catalogue record for this book is available
from the British Library

Printed and bound in the United Arab Emirates

*Happy are
those whose
refuge is in you,
whose hearts
are set on the
pilgrim ways!*

PSALM 84:5

CONTENTS

INTRODUCTION

Life is often pictured as a journey in which we travel from one given point to another – from birth to death.

But where does the journey of life lead? Most journeys are taken in order to arrive at a hoped-for destination. If the path is going to peter out in a dead end – literally – there is not much sense in making the journey.

The purpose of travelling and the final destination are supremely important in the Christian journey of life. Christian writers have loved and used the journey metaphor for centuries.

Back in the Middle Ages, William Langland pictured people on a journey in his poem 'Piers Plowman'. In the seventeenth century Bunyan wrote *The Pilgrim's Progress*, describing Christian's eventful journey from the City of Destruction to the Celestial City.

In this book I have focused on different characteristics of the journey which leads home to God, defining some of the key elements of Christian experience.

I have used remembered incidents from my early childhood as parables to throw light on each topic in turn. Some have an obvious bearing on the topic, others need a bit more thinking about. When I was three years old, my father went to London for a two-year course of training. Money was tight in those days before educational grants, so my mother and older sister and I went to live with her parents in an old-fashioned house in a seaside town. My grandparents – who grew up in the Victorian age – were devout members of a small, strict nonconformist church. I had no opportunity to meet or play with children of my own age. So my early years were very different from those of most children today. When I was five we moved near London and lived together as a family of four, with other aunts and uncles nearby. All the incidents I describe belong either to the years spent with the grandparents – when I was between three and five – or to the next few years when I was still very young.

For each section Bible verses have been selected as 'signposts', to point in the right direction. I have also chosen quotations from the writings of other Christians down the ages and across the world to light up the subjects still more. Readers should feel free to pick out those passages that seem helpful and relevant to them, and ignore the rest. We all vary in our responses and in the styles and approaches we personally find helpful. I have tried to provide a wide choice in order to suit all tastes.

Spiritual truth is different from truth in other disciplines, where proveable facts are the basis for belief. We are dealing with relationships, based on love and trust, not on scientific laws. Added to that, theologians are handling truth too great or unknowable to be boxed in by factual information alone. Because

God is far greater than we are, we cannot hope to understand everything about him. Often, as we look at different aspects of his character or his dealings with us, we seem to be faced with apparently opposite concepts. Paradox is a necessary element of Christian truth. The way forward is not to ignore or neglect one aspect but to try to hold both in tension. Only the two taken together can give us an inkling of what God is like – although full understanding is still beyond our grasp. At the end of each section I have tried to put some of these Christian paradoxes in a nutshell or picked out some other key thought for further reflection.

This book is specially intended for those who have only just set out on the Christian journey, whatever their age may be. The road is often uphill – never easy, but always challenging. As we climb higher, the air gets cleaner and fresher, the view clearer and more panoramic and the pleasure of travel more exhilarating. At whatever stage of the road you may be – whether in years or spiritual experience – I hope you will join me on this journey of the spirit.

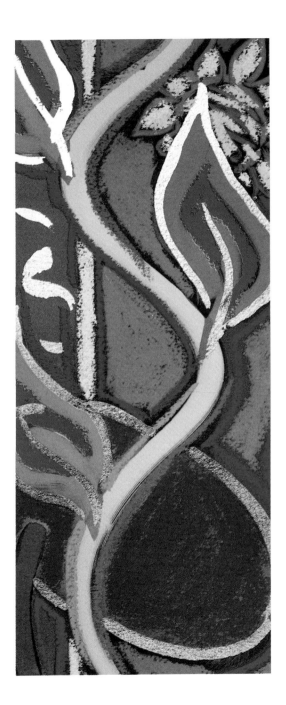

The Two Ways

When I was a very small child I would gaze up at a strange picture hanging in the hall of my grandparents' old-fashioned house. It was a mix between artistic creation and diagram, entitled 'The Two Ways'.

On one side of the picture was a wide road, bustling with extravagantly-dressed people, laughing and enjoying themselves. On the right was a narrow road, along which a few soberly-dressed men and women purposefully pursued their way. I thought that the wide road looked by far the more attractive, but I knew I was not supposed to feel that way. For at the end of the narrow road bright clouds and angel figures were poised to welcome the earnest travellers, while far ahead on the wide road billowing smoke and belching flames waited to consume the merry travellers at their journey's end.

I realize now I am older that the artist's illustration of the two ways, which caught my imagination as a child, was a very Victorian interpretation of Jesus' metaphor of the wide and narrow roads. The picture implied that happiness in the world to come is only won at the cost of dreariness and drabness now. On the other hand, any present enjoyment will be paid for later.

But the narrow road that Jesus recommended is satisfying and fulfilling in the here and now. Everlasting life is not something to be experienced only in some hazy future state; it is a rich and rewarding way of life to be enjoyed now and which will lead to even further fulfilment in the world to come. The writer of Proverbs in the Old Testament of the Bible described it as a journey from dawn into full sunshine: 'The road the righteous travel is like the sunrise, getting brighter and brighter until daylight has come.'

Not surprisingly, the road we travel with God may sometimes be tough, but those who choose it discover that it is the only road worth taking. It may not pander to our love of soft comfort or self-indulgence, but it satisfies the deepest needs and longings of the human spirit. If it is a demanding road to travel, it also provides deep joys and freedoms that the wide road never affords.

St Teresa was born in Avila in 1515 into a noble Spanish family. She became a Carmelite nun and later had a profound spiritual experience which changed her life. She was both a mystic and a highly practical woman, who reformed and founded religious houses and wrote about prayer and the life of the spirit. She has her own definition of the narrow way:

> *You pretend to make the law burdensome for us,*
> *but I do not see it as such, Lord,*
> *nor do I see how*
> *it is the narrow path that leads to you.*
> *It is not a path*
> *but a royal thoroughfare,*
> *and whoever sets out along it*
> *goes forward in the greatest safety.*
> TERESA OF AVILA (1515-82)

The Journey Beckons

FULFILMENT

At the chapel that my grandparents attended it was the custom from time to time to hold special meetings, on a Saturday or Bank Holiday. I do not remember whether, as a very small child, I was subjected to the whole afternoon's meetings. Perhaps kindly grown-ups only took me half way through. All that remains in my memory is the blessedness of the tea interval. Plates of the nicest food were handed round and I was at my happiest. This, for me, was the chief purpose of the gathering. Surprisingly, others thought differently. Some people seemed more interested in talking to each other than in eating. Others were transported by the 'messages' they had heard, scarcely aware of the tempting tea. For me, the food was the message.

Most people aim for self-fulfilment. In fact, to be fulfilled is almost considered a basic human right in a rich society. Sex, money, power, possessions, even children, are all seen as means to that goal. The word 'fulfilment' may sound nobler than self-seeking or self-indulgence, but it can be every bit as selfish and ruthless.

And oddly enough the human quest for fulfilment is often fruitless and unsatisfying. We read of people who have succeeded in becoming rich, famous and influential but whose lives bear witness to deep unhappiness and discontent. Are we getting the wrong messages about the purpose and goals in life?

Jesus made puzzling and unexpected comments on

choosing a satisfying lifestyle. He said that those who try to indulge and cosset themselves will be losers, while those willing to risk everything on his behalf find life in its truest sense. God's truth, which is stranger than fiction, is that if we stop concentrating on ourselves and our own needs, and give ourselves in love to God and to others, we discover the secret of life itself.

Many have tried the broad road of self-fulfilment and found it flat, shallow and purposeless. The narrow way of self-giving is the way to life; it yields deep joys and lasting satisfactions. The path that Jesus calls us to follow may not hold out the kind of bribes we have come to value, that touch only the surface of satisfaction. But the narrow road has a lure and attractiveness that speaks to the very heart of our being. When that road beckons, we want to answer God's call and follow it to the end. The springs of joy and contentment, peace and security are all to be discovered on the narrow road.

BIBLE SIGNPOSTS

Happy are those
 who reject the advice of evil people,
 who do not follow the example of sinners
 or join those who have no use for God.
Instead, they find joy in obeying the Law of the Lord...
They are like trees that grow beside a stream,
 that bear fruit at the right time,
 and whose leaves do not dry up.
PSALM 1:1-3

Jesus said: 'I am the light of the world. No follower of mine shall live in darkness; he shall have the light of life.'
JOHN 8:12

Jesus said: 'I have come in order that you might have life –
life in all its fullness.'
JOHN 10:10

Jesus said: 'Whoever wants to save his own life will lose it;
but whoever loses his life for me... will save it. Does a
person gain anything if he wins the whole world but loses
his life? Of course not! there is nothing he can give to
regain his life.'
MARK 8:35-37

How precious, O God, is your constant love!...
You are the source of all life,
    and because of your light we see the light.
FROM PSALM 36:7, 9

You will show me the path of life;
    in your presence is the fullness of joy,
    at your right hand are pleasures for evermore.
FROM PSALM 16:11

The Christian gospel does not offer happiness as an incentive
to its followers. But it does insist that deep fulfilment and joy
are by-products of a Christian life which may, nonetheless, be
marked by suffering, self-denial and sorrow.

In the Beatitudes (the sayings in the Gospels that begin
with 'blessed are...'), Jesus recognized that true contentment
and satisfaction do not belong to the rich, the powerful or the
self-indulgent. They are the hallmark of those who set out on
quite different quests and who put God first. Such people are
not generally considered successful or to be envied. They are
prepared to enter into the pain and sorrow of others. They
strive hard for goodness, justice and peace in their own lives
and in our world. They put loyalty to Jesus before personal
comfort or safety.

The word 'blessed' in the Beatitudes has also been
translated 'to be congratulated'. Jesus is describing not so

much the subjective feeling of happiness as the kind of people who are the real achievers – in God's eyes. Here, says Jesus, are the people who have found the secret of life. They may weep, be exhausted or even hounded to death, but they have the key to true blessedness in God's sight. They put God first and respond with his love to a world in need. They do not look for superficial, passing enjoyment, but discover a deep well of contentment and peace in the never-failing resources of a loving, eternal God and a life lived in close touch with him.

TRAVELLERS' TALES

The word blessed which is used in each of the beatitudes is the Greek word makarios. The meaning of makarios can best be seen from one particular usage of it. The Greeks always called Cyprus he makaria which means The Happy Isle, and they did so because they believed that Cyprus was so lovely, so rich, and so fertile an island that a man would never need to go beyond its coastline to find the perfectly happy life. Makarios then describes that joy which has its secret within itself, that joy which is serene and untouchable, and self-contained, that joy which is completely independent of all the chances and the changes of life... which... sorrow and loss, and pain and grief, are powerless to touch... which nothing in life or death can take away.... The Christian has the serene and untouchable joy which comes from walking for ever in the company and in the presence of Jesus Christ.... In the face of the beatitudes a gloom-encompassed Christianity is unthinkable.

FROM COMMENTARY ON ST MATTHEW'S GOSPEL, DAILY STUDY BIBLE,
PROFESSOR WILLIAM BARCLAY

Blessed are the poor...
not the penniless
but those whose heart is free.

Blessed are those who mourn...
not those who whimper
but those who raise their voices.

Blessed are the meek...
not the soft
but those who are patient and tolerant.

Blessed are those who hunger and thirst for justice...
not those who whine
but those who struggle.

Blessed are the merciful...
not those who forget
but those who forgive.

Blessed are the pure in heart...
not those who act like angels
but those whose life is transparent.

Blessed are those who are persecuted for justice...
not because they suffer
but because they love.

COMPARTIR SANTIAGO, P. JACOB, CHILE

O thou who dost direct my feet
To right or left where pathways part,
Wilt thou not, faithful Paraclete,
Direct the journeying of my heart?

This is the road of my desire –
Learning to love as God loves me,
Ready to pass through flood or fire
With Christ's unwearying constancy.

FRANK HOUGHTON (1894-1972), 'ROAD OF MY DESIRE'

FOR REFLECTION

The road to true fulfilment leads to God, the source of all joy.

Starting Out

CHOICE

One day, when my mother and I were out shopping, we went into a jeweller's shop. While she talked to the shopkeeper I looked at the lovely, shining things for sale. As the shopkeeper talked she kept turning from my mother to look at me. Later my mother explained why she was so interested in me. I reminded her of her own little girl who had died when she was three or four – the age that I was then.

When she had finished telling my mother her sad story she turned to me and said, 'You may choose anything you like from the shop for yourself.' It was a child's dream come true.

My mother looked at the expensive, genuine but discreet pieces for sale, then at the cheap, gaudy, costume jewellery set out in trays on the counter. She willed me to choose wisely, but could not interfere and tell me what was worth having. Not surprisingly, I picked out a glittering, cheap paste imitation for my gift. I was not wise enough to know the fake from the genuine article.

Life is full of choices. Most of them are unimportant, but others can change the whole course of our lives. Sometimes we don't even seem to be making a choice. We choose by default. We are so engrossed in the various concerns of our busy lives that we fail to reach out for what is so much more worth having, and could be ours for the choosing. But many people are beginning to discover that when life is crammed full with work, leisure, entertainment, sport, social companionship, and nothing more, we have been fobbed off with something less than human life was meant to contain.

Jesus said that we 'cannot live by bread alone'. We need 'every word that God speaks'. Life with no spiritual dimension lacks the most important ingredient of human experience. Without God, there is an emptiness that nothing else can fill. Not everyone is aware of the missing factor but many are deeply conscious of a lack of meaning to life. They feel as if they are drifting without purpose. Others recognize that they do not have the resources in themselves to cope with their failings or to deal with the pressures they face. Many have experienced the breakdown of relationships and are desperately disillusioned and lonely.

Jesus is described in the Bible as bread for the hungry, water for the thirsty, the door that leads to fullness of life. If we are aware that we need more than bread – the satisfaction of material needs – we can find the answer to unsatisfied longing in close relationship with Jesus, who is called God's living Word.

Over the last two thousand years millions of people have discovered that choosing to follow Jesus Christ is the best choice anyone can make in life. As time goes by, Jesus becomes more precious, more real and more central to the people whose lives he enters. But first we need to know something about this person who is the very centre of the Christian faith.

JESUS

The Bible tells us that Jesus was born in the same way every child is born, yet he was different from all others. Uniquely he was both God and man. He combined in one nature real humanity and deity. As man he was able to understand and enter our life experiences and as Son of God he had the power to rescue us from the mess human beings have made of things.

Jesus grew up in obscurity in an ordinary working family. It was not until he was thirty that he set out as a travelling teacher and preacher in his home country of Israel. With his coming, he said, the kingdom – or rule – of God had arrived. The Jewish nation, through whom God had made known his laws and his love, was eagerly awaiting the time when God's rule would usher in permanent peace and justice. They were longing for political independence and freedom from the occupying Roman forces. But Jesus did not come to set up an earthly kingdom. 'God's kingdom' would be established in the lives of those who gladly recognized his right to rule and to determine their destiny.

Jesus was no ordinary teacher. He backed up the claims he made with the deeds he did. He healed the sick and disabled, brought back the dead to life and even showed his control over storms and rough seas – actions which demonstrated his God-given authority and power. Perhaps even more amazingly, no one was ever able to point to any faults in him. He lived a life entirely free from wrongdoing, always obedient to God, his Father. In his teaching and lifestyle he demonstrated a new way of living and relating to others, based on love and forgiveness.

His teaching enthralled the ordinary people who flocked to hear him. But it antagonized some of the established teachers and leaders. After about three years of public teaching and healing he was arrested, given a mockery of a trial and put to death by crucifixion – an unbelievably cruel method of execution.

But Jesus was not the helpless victim of human treachery and prejudice. Long before it happened, he had told his followers that he would lay down his life voluntarily. He was going to die on behalf of others, taking on himself the wrongs and failures and rebellion of all humanity against God. Through his death he would make a bridge of forgiveness, reconciling men and women to God. His death was not the end. As he had predicted, he would live again, having conquered evil and death itself – the final enemy. He would open up a new way to God, a journey of the spirit, for all who trust him and give him supreme place in their lives.

In Jesus God broke into history and entered our world at a given time and place. He has promised to break into history again, when Jesus returns at some unknown date to establish peace and justice and to judge the world.

BIBLE SIGNPOSTS

Jesus said: 'The kingdom of Heaven is like treasure which a man found buried in a field. He buried it again, and in joy went and sold everything he had, and bought the field.

'Again, the kingdom of heaven is like this. A merchant looking out for fine pearls found one of very special value; so he went and sold everything he had and bought it.'
MATTHEW 13:44-46

Joshua said to the people: 'Choose for yourselves this day whom you will serve... But as for me and my household, we will serve the Lord.'
JOSHUA 24:14-15

These are the words of the Lord: 'I offer you now a choice between the way of life and the way of death.'
JEREMIAH 21:8

When we choose to commit our lives to Christ we make the biggest and most important decision of our lives. Some think that the choice is too costly, but to have Jesus is worth everything else we might have to sacrifice. Too often the Christian life has been depicted in a negative way – as if it were a matter of going without and giving up things. But what we gain is infinitely more important and more satisfying than anything else. Jesus promises to give us life – life in all its fullness. When Jesus – not self – is the mainspring of life, we become more truly human than we can ever be by living for ourselves. He gives purpose, direction, meaning and adventure to our existence. He brings us forgiveness, peace, freedom, love, and life that will last beyond death.

God has given us the freedom to choose or reject Jesus. But

when we choose Jesus we can also know for certain that God has already chosen us. He chose us to belong to him before our world was made. It is hard for us with our limited human understanding to reconcile these two seemingly opposite viewpoints, but both are true. We find 'hidden treasure' and 'the pearl of great price' when we find Jesus; then we discover that God values us as treasure too. He has chosen us, his dearly loved children, to become part of his family. In Jesus, we find our true destiny. We are men and women already loved and accepted by God.

TRAVELLERS' TALES

Yevgeni Pushkov, a Russian music student born in 1941, brought up to accept atheism and materialism, still searched for truth:

> I would like to tell you about how I found happiness in the Lord Jesus Christ.
> More than once I asked myself the question: 'What is the purpose of life in the end? What am I living for?'
> One day I came across these words written by the great German composer, Wagner: 'Music cannot be an end in itself: music is only a means of expressing an end.' But what kind of elusive 'end' could this be? I had to ask myself, do I have a purpose in life? There was no answer – for I knew that I had none.
> To find an answer to those questions which now tormented me, I became engrossed in science. Perhaps there I could discover real truth. But I found no comfort there... Again and again I asked myself, 'How can I find out what the real truth is?' But not a living soul could ever give me a satisfactory answer. No one could say to me: 'I am the truth. I teach the truth.'
> And then, I found it. Only one book in the world contained the answer to my question. That book was the Bible. There in the pages of John's Gospel I read those comforting words, the words of Jesus Christ himself: 'I am

the way, the truth, and the life.'
FROM LIGHT THROUGH THE CURTAIN

Fount of all life, dancing in bliss,
Breaking down walls, making new space.

Burning up evil, creating afresh,
Calling your people, follow in faith.

Living with Jesus, power in his Name,
Healing the broken, restoring the lame.

Casting out demons, raising the dead,
Calming life's storms, removing all dread.

Living to serve, confirmed from above,
Tested by fire, aflame with God's love.

Seeking the lost, sharing all pain,
Love at such cost, rising again.

Lighting our path, dancing ahead,
Leading through death, lifting to life.
UNITED THEOLOGICAL COLLEGE, BANGALORE

He is a path, if any be misled;
He is a robe, if any naked be;
If any chance to hunger, he is bread;
If any be a bondman, he is free;
If any be but weak, how strong is he!
    To dead men life he is, to sick men health;
    To blind men sight, and to the needy wealth,
A pleasure without loss, a treasure without stealth.
GILES FLETCHER (1586-1623)

FOR REFLECTION

God chose me to be his before he made the world. Yet, just as certainly, I choose to follow him.

The Way In

HUMILITY

*My grandmother was a fine needlewoman and I
decided that I would like to sew too. So she used to provide
me with small squares of material and a needle ready
threaded. Then she offered to show me how to sew neatly
round the edges. But I wanted to do it all by myself. I am
not sure exactly what went wrong or how the threads got
caught up; I only know that however hard I tried, I always
ended up with a tight little ball of material. My grandmother
gently offered to rescue me and restore the sewing but I
refused. Rather than admit that I had gone wrong and could
not manage alone, I pretended that the tight ball of material
was exactly what I had set out to make. My grandmother
never said a word but I think I knew then that I did not
deceive her any more than I did myself. I was not the sort of
child Jesus referred to as a pattern of humility.*

Most of us learn to put on a good front to hide our
vulnerability. In our competitive world the weak seem so often
to go to the wall, so we dare not admit our weaknesses or our
need of others. We must be tough, self-sufficient and confident
in order to succeed.

Jesus said that in order to start on the road that leads to
life we must go through a small gate. If we are to squeeze
through there will be no room for the baggage of self-
sufficiency, self-seeking or self-satisfaction that many of us
carry around with us. We have to leave behind all pretence, all
love of our own way and all that false independence which sees
trust in God as a crutch for the weak.

BIBLE SIGNPOSTS

Jesus said: 'Blessed is the person who has realized his own utter helplessness, and who has put his whole trust in God.'

PROFESSOR WILLIAM BARCLAY'S RENDERING OF MATTHEW 5:3

The disciples came to Jesus and asked, 'Who is the greatest in the kingdom of heaven?' He called a child, set him in front of them, and said, 'Truly I tell you: unless you turn round and become like children, you will never enter the kingdom of heaven. Whoever humbles himself and becomes like this child will be the greatest in the kingdom of heaven.'

MATTHEW 18:1-4

No place is left for any human pride in the presence of God. By God's act you are in Christ Jesus; God has made him our wisdom, and in him we have our righteousness, our holiness, our liberation.

1 CORINTHIANS 1:29-30

When Jesus talks about being humble he does not mean that the Christian way is for those with a poor sense of self-worth. He means that we need to be cut down to size – to recognize our smallness and God's greatness – if we are to set off on the narrow road. It is only with a sense of need and reliance upon God that we are able to go in through the gate that leads to the royal highway.

Jesus himself is the way to God. It is through him and only through him that we can begin on the journey to life. Our society offers a range of products which claim to bring spiritual satisfaction. It implies that no one way is better than another. So it takes humility to accept that Jesus is the one non-optional way to God. The journey of the spirit begins with him.

Travellers' Tales

Perhaps the challenge of the gospel lies precisely in the invitation to accept a gift for which we can give nothing in return.

HENRI NOUWEN

We are all beggars before God.

MARTIN LUTHER (1483-1546)

William Law was a gentle and respected teacher and writer. In the days when larks and linnets were sold in cages, he would buy them in order to set them free. Dr Johnson and the Wesley brothers were among those greatly influenced by Law's best-known book, *A Serious Call to a Devout and Holy Life*, where he writes:

> *Humility does not consist of having a worse opinion of ourselves than we deserve, or in abasing ourselves lower than we really are. No... humility is founded in a true and just sense of our weakness, misery and sin.*
>
> WILLIAM LAW (1686-1761)

Carlo Carretto, who died in 1988, was a devout man who led a Christian centre near Assisi in Italy. He journeyed to the desert to learn to pray:

> *For so many years, for too many years, I have fought against my powerlessness, my weakness. Often I have refused to admit it to myself, preferring to appear in public with a nice mask of self-assurance.*
>
> *It is pride which will not let us admit this powerlessness; pride which won't let us accept being inadequate. God has made me understand this, little by little.*
>
> *Now I don't fight any more; I try to accept myself. I try to face up to myself without illusions, dreams or*

28

fantasies. It's a step forward, I believe... Now I contrast my powerlessness with the powerfulness of God, the heap of my sins with the completeness of God's mercy, and I place the abyss of my smallness beneath the abyss of his greatness...

And this meeting between God's totality and man's nothingness is the greatest wonder of creation... Really, it is the truth of God and man. The acceptance of this truth comes from humility, and that is why without humility there is no truth, and without truth no humility.

FROM *LETTERS FROM THE DESERT*, CARLO CARRETTO

FOR REFLECTION

Whatever my age, I must enter God's kingdom as a child.

The Cost of the Journey

COMMITMENT

One day, when I was small, I set my heart on washing all the breakfast dishes, by myself. I was ready to give all I had to this interesting and worthwhile cause. I put on a pinafore, and pulled across a box to stand on, so that I would be tall enough to reach the sink. Soon I was up to my elbows in soapy suds and dirty dishes.

I began enthusiastically but I had not reckoned with the size of the task. Soon I began to grow tired and the pile of dishes seemed just as big. Tears rolled down my cheeks as I struggled on. It was then that my father came along. He saw at once what was happening and gently suggested that he should give me a hand. I was no longer too proud to accept help, and I gladly let him share the work with me. Together we finished the job.

Commitment is not a popular word today. It seems safer not to make promises we may be unable or unwilling to keep. The cost is too high; our independence and freedom to act might be curtailed. When the commitment is to a person rather than a cause, we may be afraid of the risks we take. Many have experienced the pain of broken marriages. It seems safer not to enter into binding relationships than risk disillusionment and suffering.

When we commit ourselves to following Jesus we are entering into a relationship with someone who is utterly reliable and trustworthy. He will never go back on his promises or his commitment to us. What is more, when the way seems too hard and we feel like giving up, Jesus is not just a helpless onlooker. He is there for us, ready to absorb our anxiety and give us the help and strength that we need to complete the journey we have begun.

BIBLE SIGNPOSTS

As soon as they had brought the boats to land, [Simon Peter, James and John] left everything and followed him.

Later, when he went out, [Jesus] saw a tax-collector, Levi by name, at his seat in the custom-house, and said to him, 'Follow me.' Leaving everything, he got up and followed him.
LUKE 5:11,27-28

I reckon everything as complete loss for the sake of what is so much more valuable, the knowledge of Christ Jesus my Lord. For his sake I have thrown everything away; I consider it all as mere refuse, so that I may gain Christ and be completely united with him.
PHILEMON 3:8-9

If we are faithless, he will remain faithful, for he cannot disown himself.
2 TIMOTHY 2:11

The good news of the gospel is that eternal life – the life that comes from God and belongs to God – is his free gift to all who are prepared to accept it. When we receive that free gift, we also pledge ourselves to follow Jesus. And Jesus never pretended that commitment to him is an easy option. He warned would-be followers that the ultimate price of such loyalty might be suffering and even death. Yet in spite of that, men and women down the ages and across the globe have made that commitment and discovered new life and true joy in giving themselves unreservedly to God. To give for Christ's sake is always to receive, and loss becomes great gain.

Some people hesitate to follow Jesus, not because he might fail them but because they might fail him. They are afraid that

31

they could never meet the requirements. But we do not have to live the Christian life simply by our own efforts. We do not have to go it alone. The Holy Spirit – the Helper Jesus promised to send – is with us to help us to keep our promises and to do what God wants.

TRAVELLERS' TALES

Dietrich Bonhoeffer, a German pastor and scholar, was hanged in a Gestapo prison in 1945 for his opposition to Hitler. When war broke out he could have remained safely in the USA where he was lecturing. But he believed it was his duty to return to Germany, where he was imprisoned. His letters and papers from prison have helped and inspired many Christians since.

You must never doubt that I am travelling my appointed road with gratitude and cheerfulness. My past life is replete with God's goodness, and my sins are covered by the forgiving love of Christ crucified. I am thankful for all those who have crossed my path, and all I wish is never to cause them sorrow, and that they like me will always be thankful for the forgiveness and mercy of God and sure of it. Please don't for a moment get upset by all this, but let it rejoice your heart.
LETTER TO A FRIEND, 23 AUGUST 1944, FROM *LETTERS AND PAPERS FROM PRISON*

Ignatius was bishop of Antioch in the second century. He wrote several letters while he was on his way to Rome where he was finally martyred, probably in 107AD.

No power, human or spiritual, must hinder my coming to Jesus Christ. So whether the way be fire, or crucifixion, or wild beasts in the arena, or the mangling of my whole body, I can bear it, provided I am assured it is the way to him.

And it is! All the riches and power in the world cannot compare with that. As far as I am concerned, to die in Jesus Christ is better than to be king of the whole wide world! Do not

try to tempt me to stay here by offering me the world and its attractions. Just let me make my way upward to that pure and undiluted light. For only when I get there will I truly be a man.
IGNATIUS OF ANTIOCH (C.35-107 AD)

On 8 January, 1956, Jim Elliot, an American Bible translator, was killed by the Auca Indians he and his colleagues were trying to evangelize. Here is his prayer:

God, I pray thee, light these idle sticks of my life and may I burn for thee. Consume my life, my God, for it is thine. I seek not a long life, but a full one, like you, Lord Jesus.
FROM SHADOW OF THE ALMIGHTY, ELIZABETH ELLIOT

O Jesus, I have promised
to serve thee to the end;
Be thou for ever near me,
My Master and my Friend;
I shall not fear the battle
If thou art by my side,
Nor wander from the pathway
If thou wilt be my Guide.

O let me see thy footmarks,
And in them plant mine own;
My hope to follow duly
Is in thy strength alone;
O guide me, call me, draw me,
Uphold me to the end;
And then in heaven receive me,
My Saviour and my Friend.
JOHN BODE (1816-74), WRITTEN FOR THE CONFIRMATION OF HIS THREE CHILDREN

FOR REFLECTION

New life in Jesus is free. But to follow him may cost everything I have.

Travelling With Confidence

FAITH

When my father was training in London he could only afford to visit us for an occasional weekend. I longed for those times. It is hard for a three year old to remember anyone for long. But once my father had arrived he was gloriously real again.

When it was time for him to go and his train was due to leave, I became tearful. Then he would always say, 'If I don't go, I can't come back.' I felt sure there was something wrong with this logic, but I could never work out what it was. I only knew that for the foreseeable future I had to live without him. But I was certain that he would come back. I could trust him utterly. He would keep his word.

Christian faith is widely misunderstood. 'I wish I had your faith!' people remark longingly to someone who is able to trust God in difficult circumstances. But faith is not the result of a talent we are born with or something in our genes. It is a deliberate and rational decision of mind and will to put our trust in God and his promises.

Faith is not blind – quite the opposite. Faith sees what is hidden from unbelieving eyes. It is not based on scientific proof, but as in any loving relationship, it is built on trust, constantly reinforced by experience.

BIBLE SIGNPOSTS

To have faith is to be sure of the things we hope for, to be certain of the things we cannot see.

No one can please God without faith, for whoever comes to God must have faith that God exists and rewards those who seek him.

HEBREWS 11:1, 6

Paul said: 'I know whom I have trusted, and I am sure that he is able to keep safe until that Day what I have entrusted to him.'

2 TIMOTHY 1:12

Though you have never seen Jesus, yet I know that you love him. At present you trust him without being able to see him, and even now he brings you a joy that words cannot express.

1 PETER 1:8

We walk by faith, not by sight.

2 CORINTHIANS 5:7

Jesus said [to Thomas], 'Because you have seen me you have found faith. Happy are they who find faith without seeing me.'

JOHN 20:29

Faith launches us on our journey of the spirit, when we accept the existence of God and believe that he has made himself known to us in Jesus. We rest all our confidence on the promises of God. We believe that he can give us forgiveness, freedom and new life. That is the beginning.

The more we come to know God and the further we go on our Christian journey, the more our faith grows, as we discover that God is utterly trustworthy. We take each step of the way trusting in him and we believe that he will guide us safely to the end of the road. Then we shall see him: faith will give place to sight.

But because we are human, our faith does not always remain constant. Sometimes it is difficult to believe that God is in control. But whatever our moods or our circumstances, we can hold on to God's promises in the Bible and by an act of mind and will, we can put our trust in him.

TRAVELLERS' TALES

The friendly night is an image of faith... a point lost in infinite space, wrapped round by the night under the subdued light of the stars. I am this point lost in space: the darkness, like an irreplaceable friend, is faith. The stars, God's witness.

When my faith was weak, all this would have seemed incomprehensible to me. I was afraid as a child is of the night. But now I have conquered it , and it is mine... The darkness is necessary, the darkness of faith is necessary, for God's light is too great. It wounds.

I understand more and more that faith is not a mysterious and cruel trick of a God who hides himself without telling me why, but is a necessary veil.

FROM *LETTERS FROM THE DESERT*, CARLO CARRETTO

Faith's substance is our will; its manner is, that we take hold on Christ by divine instinct; its final cause and fruit, that it purifies the heart, makes us children of God, and brings with it the remission of sins. Faith is not only necessary, that thereby the ungodly may become justified and saved before God, and their hearts be settled in peace, but it is necessary in every other respect. St Paul says: 'Now that we are justified by faith, we have peace with God through our Lord Jesus Christ.'

FROM *TABLE TALK*, MARTIN LUTHER (1483-1546)

Wednesday May 24 1738: In the evening I went very unwillingly to a society in Aldersgate Street, where one was reading from Luther's preface to the Epistle to the Romans. About a quarter before nine, while he was describing the change which God works in the heart through faith in Christ, I felt my heart strangely warmed. I felt I did trust in Christ, Christ alone, for salvation; and an assurance was given me that he had taken away my sins, even mine, and saved me from the law of sin and death.

FROM *THE JOURNAL OF JOHN WESLEY*

No coward soul is mine,
No trembler in the world's storm-troubled sphere:
I see Heaven's glories shine,
And faith shines equal, arming me from fear.

FROM THE 'LAST LINES' OF EMILY BRONTË (1818-48)

FOR REFLECTION

Putting the weight of our trust on what is unseen gives our lives steadiness and certainty.

Knowing the Way

CERTAINTY AND DOUBT

One day my mother told us we were going on a train and that our father would meet us at the other end. I was enormously excited and when at last we arrived I scarcely stopped to look twice at the tall, dark man waiting to welcome us at the station. I hurled myself into his arms. He hugged and kissed me back, and it was a full minute before I realized that it was not my father. I had made a terrible mistake. At the last minute he had been unable to come and his brother had met us instead. In floods of tears I broke away from the arms of this uncle I had never met before, and refused all his attempts to comfort me. My father arrived later and I soon came to know and love the uncle who looked so like him. But that day I discovered that doubt as well as certainty is a necessary ingredient of life.

The earliest statement of belief required of new Christian converts was probably nothing more than 'Jesus is Lord'. It was two hundred years or more before a fuller creed was required at baptism. But 'Jesus is Lord' implies a great deal about who Jesus is and how he changes a person's lifestyle.

The early Christians lived at a time when those within the Roman Empire were obliged to take an oath of allegiance to the Emperor, saying 'Caesar is Lord'. In so doing they were asserting Caesar's divinity and his right over their lives. It is not surprising that many Christians faced torture and death rather than take this oath. They had another allegiance. When they said 'Jesus is Lord' they were affirming that he is God and that he had complete right over their lives.

BIBLE SIGNPOSTS

If the confession 'Jesus is Lord' is on your lips, and the faith that God raised him from the dead is in your heart, you will find salvation.
ROMANS 10:9

For I am convinced that there is nothing... in all creation that can separate us from the love of God in Christ Jesus our Lord.
ROMANS 8:38-39

Here is a saying you may trust, one that merits full acceptance: 'Christ Jesus came into the world to save sinners'.
1 TIMOTHY 1:15

I passed on to you what I received, which is of the greatest importance: that Christ died for our sins, as written in the Scriptures; that he was buried and that he was raised to life three days later, as written in the Scriptures... this is what we all preach, and this is what you believe.
1 CORINTHIANS 15:3-4,11

At present we see only puzzling reflections in a mirror, but one day we shall see face to face. My knowledge now is partial; then it will be whole, like God's knowledge of me.
1 CORINTHIANS 13:12

I did not understand you.
Yet I always stay close to you,
and you hold me by the hand.
PSALM 73:22-23

The New Testament is uncompromising on the basic tenets of our faith. Christianity rests on rock-solid facts. Most of these concern Jesus – his death and resurrection and the central place God has given him. Just as certain is God's unconditional love for us, as well as his holiness and justice. Christians from all traditions are at one in affirming these foundational beliefs.

But there are other areas where we have to be content to keep an open mind and to admit humbly but trustingly that we don't know. We may be able to recite the Christian statements of belief, but we cannot always understand how they work out in practice. We cannot satisfactorily explain God and his ways, either to ourselves or to others. We can only admit that God is too great for us to comprehend. If we could completely understand and explain God, he would not be any greater than our own human minds.

Doubts may not be only in the mind. There are times when our hopes and feelings are crushed. God seems far away and the bottom seems to have dropped out of life because of what is happening to us or to others in our world. How can we reconcile a loving God with some of the injustice and suffering we witness, or experience ourselves? At such times we can only hold on to the things that are certain until the mist lifts and the way ahead is a little clearer. However it may seem, we know that God does love us and that he is in ultimate control. Even when the mists don't clear, we can go on trusting – walking by faith, not sight – certain, because of our loving relationship with him, that God still loves us and is with us whatever may happen.

Travellers' Tales

As a young man George Fox, founder of the Society of Friends, consulted ministers and preachers in vain, in an earnest attempt to find a faith that satisfied him. At last, in 1647, he said:

When my hopes in them and in all men were gone, so that I had nothing outwardly to help me, nor could tell what to do, then, oh then, I heard a voice which said, 'There is one, even Christ Jesus, that can speak to thy condition,' and when I heard it, my heart did leap for joy.

Father,
I am seeking:

I am hesitant and uncertain,
but will you, O God,
watch over each step of mine
and guide me.

FROM CONFESSIONS, AUGUSTINE OF HIPPO (354-430)

Looking at ourselves and our certainty as ours, we discover its weakness, its vulnerability to every critical thought... But looking at God we realize that all the shortcomings of our experience are of no importance. Looking at God, we see that we do not have him as an object of our knowledge, but that he has us as the subject of our existence. Looking at God, we feel that we cannot escape him even by making him an object of sceptical arguments or of irresistible emotions. We realize that in our uncertainty there is one fixed point of certainty, however we may name it and describe it and explain it.

FROM THE NEW BEING, PAUL TILLICH

Bishop John Robinson became widely known in the Sixties for his controversial book *Honest to God*. Shortly before his death in 1983, he described his faith in this way:

When people ask me what is the hard centre of my faith I sometimes sum it up by saying 'The grace of our Lord Jesus Christ, and the love of God and the fellowship of the Holy Spirit.' You can't put it more succinctly than that. It is those realities, as the ultimate environment in which we live, which seem to me to be the things we have to make real and to find expression for and to live in... I see them in terms of personal relationship and personal trust, both with God and through other people and in other people. That is the reality by which I actually seek to live and those are the things that actually keep me going.

FROM DRAWING NEAR TO THE CITY, SHELAGH BROWN

FOR REFLECTION

I may not always understand God's ways but I can safely trust him.

The Freedom of the Road

TRUE FREEDOM

It was a summer Sunday evening and the sea below was calm and inviting. I stood on the outskirts of the open-air meeting that my grandfather and his 'brothers' from the chapel were holding on the Overcliff Drive. Before it had finished my grandmother decided to go home and gently asked me to go with her. I shook my head, determined to stay longer. She did not try to persuade me and she and my mother walked quietly away. I can still remember the pain that wrenched my heart as I watched their retreating figures. I longed to be safely between them, loved and guided home. I had asserted my independence but the price had been too high. I would have felt freer and happier going with them in loving obedience than having my own way.

Many people see themselves as victims: they can't help the way they are because of their upbringing, their education or their genes. They have never known real freedom. Others lose their freedom through some form of addiction, or are controlled by their ambitions and desires.

Jesus promised to set people free. He can break the power of the things that imprison us. He does not do this by imposing harsh rules or prohibitions. He sets us free from the things that have been enslaving us by offering us his love and forgiveness. It is in this new relationship of love and service to him that we find true freedom.

BIBLE SIGNPOSTS

Jesus said: 'If you obey my teaching, you are really my disciples; you will know the truth, and the truth will set you free... I am telling you the truth: everyone who sins is the slave of sin... If the Son sets you free, then you will be really free.'

JOHN 8:31-36

For freedom Christ has set us free; stand fast therefore, and do not submit again to a yoke of slavery.

GALATIANS 5:1

By the death of Christ we are set free, that is, our sins are forgiven.

EPHESIANS 1:7

Live as those who are free; not however as though your freedom provided a cloak for wrongdoing, but as slaves in God's service.

1 PETER 2:16

When we put ourselves in God's hands, he wants to set us free from the hurts and hates and bad actions of the past. He gently loosens the chains of guilt and heals our pain. This does not always happen overnight. It is sometimes a long process. When we give up the right to have our own way and hand over control to Jesus, we are not exchanging one harsh taskmaster for another. Jesus sets us free within a relationship of love. We choose to go his way because we love him and long to please him.

TRAVELLERS' TALES

In 1986 Amnesty International reported that there were probably over five thousand prisoners held near the centre of

Addis Ababa in a prison called 'The End of the World'. One third of them were political prisoners. One woman, an inmate for five years, wrote down her meditations for fellow-prisoners. She commented: 'When visitors came to see us I also saw supposedly "free" people who appeared to be prisoners of their own bars... I asked myself why I felt much freer than these people.'

> *There is no one more... appreciative of the magic word liberty than a prisoner. But it is one thing to recognize bondage when thrown behind bars, and another to recognize the bondage of sin... Once we know the Lord then we are free, behind bars or outside. Freedom is within ourselves – there are many who have created their own bars. We can truly be free if we know and walk with the Lord.*
> FROM *THE PRISONER'S LANTERN*

> *If you would find freedom, learn above all to discipline your senses and your soul. Be not led hither and thither by your desires and your members. Keep your spirit and your body chaste, wholly subject to you, and obediently seeking the goal that is set before you. None can learn the secret of freedom, save by discipline.*
> FROM *STATIONS ON THE ROAD TO FREEDOM*, DIETRICH BONHOEFFER

> *A Christian is a perfectly free lord of all, subject to none. A Christian is a perfectly dutiful servant of all, subject to all.*
> FROM *THE FREEDOM OF A CHRISTIAN*, MARTIN LUTHER (1483-1546)

> *Make me a captive, Lord,*
> *And then I shall be free;*
> *Force me to render up my sword,*
> *And I shall conqueror be.*
> *I sink in life's alarms*
> *When by myself I stand;*
> *Imprison me within thine arms,*
> *And strong shall be my hand.*

My heart is weak and poor
Until it master find:
It has no spring of action sure,
It varies with the wind.
It cannot freely move
Till thou hast wrought its chain,
Enslave it with thy matchless love,
And deathless it shall reign.

GEORGE MATHESON (1842-1906)

FOR REFLECTION

In serving God I find perfect freedom.

Shedding the Load

FORGIVENESS

When we lived with our grandparents I had to be polite to their grown-up friends. One visitor, with the unfortunate name of William Nutter, I found hard to bear. Once when he called I hid behind the sofa. My grandmother tried to coax me to come out, especially as Mr Nutter had brought me a present. It was an empty book of stamps in which he had stuck Bible texts. He described this gift to lure me out but I was not tempted.

After he had gone I emerged, and the moment I saw the distress on my grandmother's face I was truly sorry. I had not realized that I had hurt her. I could not bear to see her looking so discomfited. I rushed into her arms in true repentance. I knew she would forgive me and love me still.

If we wish to travel light on our journey to God, we need to shed the twin loads of guilt and an unforgiving spirit. A sense of guilt is the cause of much unhappiness and depression, but the Christian has no need to go on carrying it. When we first see ourselves as God sees us it is right to feel guilty that we have deliberately flouted him and chosen to go our own way. But when we turn to God in trust and commitment, we experience his free forgiveness. Jesus took the load of our wrongdoing when he died on our behalf. We can go forward into a new life, without the dragging weight of guilt and remorse. And when we go wrong in the future, we can come to him again for forgiveness. God is ready to forgive and accept us.

BIBLE SIGNPOSTS

God puts people right through their faith in Jesus Christ. God does this to all who believe in Christ, because there is no

difference at all: everyone has sinned and is far away from God's saving presence. But by the free gift of God's grace all are put right with him through Christ Jesus, who sets them free.
ROMANS 3:22-24

If we claim to be without sin, we deceive ourselves and the truth is not in us. If we confess our sins, he is faithful and just to forgive us our sins and to purify us from all unrighteousness.
1 JOHN 1:8-9

It is through Christ, at the cost of his own blood, that we are redeemed, freely forgiven through that full and generous grace which has overflowed into our lives.
EPHESIANS 1:7

Jesus linked being forgiven by God with forgiving others. The Lord's Prayer reminds us that we ask for God's forgiveness when we are ready to forgive those who have wronged us. Some of us may have been gravely wronged and it seems almost impossible to forgive. But if we refuse to forgive others we block up the channel by which we can receive God's forgiveness. To put it in terms of our journey, we carry a weight that will impede us on our road to God. We become hard and bitter and unable to develop as Christians and as human beings. Failure to forgive is destructive. It hurts the one who bears the grudge more than the one who has done the wrong. It is impossible sometimes to forgive by our own efforts, but once we are willing to forgive, God will help us to do what we cannot do simply by our own efforts.

Peter came to Jesus and asked, 'Lord, if my brother keeps on sinning against me, how many times do I have to forgive him? Seven times?'
'No, not seven times,' answered Jesus, 'but seventy times seven'.
MATTHEW 18:21-22

Jesus said: 'When you stand praying, if you have a grievance against anyone, forgive him, so that your Father in heaven may forgive you the wrongs you have done.'

MARK 11:25

Be generous to one another, tender-hearted, forgiving one another as God in Christ forgave you.

EPHESIANS 4:32

TRAVELLERS' TALES

In John Bunyan's *Pilgrim's Progress*, Christian set out on his journey to the Celestial City with a heavy burden on his back – the burden of his sin and guilt:

Now I saw in my dream, that the highway up which Christian was to go, was fenced on either side with a Wall, and that Wall is called Salvation. Up this way therefore did burdened Christian run, but not without great difficulty, because of the load on his back.

He ran thus till he came to a place somewhat ascending; and upon that place stood a Cross, and a little below in the bottom, a sepulchre. So I saw in my dream, that just as Christian came up with the Cross, his burden loosed from his shoulders, and fell from off his back; and began to tumble, and so continued to do till it came to the mouth of the sepulchre, where it fell in, and I saw it no more.

Then was Christian glad and lightsome, and said with a merry heart, 'He hath given me rest, by his sorrow, and life, by his death'.

Forgiveness is not an occasional act; it is a permanent attitude.

FROM *STRENGTH TO LOVE*, MARTIN LUTHER KING

Corrie ten Boom, a watchmaker's daughter living in Holland at the outbreak of World War II, hid Jewish people from German arrest. As a result, her family was arrested and she and her sister were eventually taken to Ravensbruck where Betsie died as the result of bad conditions and ill-treatment. After her release, Corrie preached in many countries, including Germany:

> *It was at a church service in Munich that I saw him, the former SS man who had stood guard at the shower room door in the processing centre at Ravensbruck. He was the first of our actual jailers that I had seen since that time. And suddenly it was all there – the roomful of mocking men, the heaps of clothing, Betsie's pain-blanched face.*
>
> *He came up to me as the church was emptying, beaming and bowing. 'How grateful I am for your message, Fraulein,' he said. 'To think that, as you say, he has washed my sins away.'*
>
> *His hand was thrust out to shake mine. And I, who had preached so often to the people in Bloemendaal the need to forgive, kept my hand at my side.*
>
> *Even as the angry, vengeful thoughts boiled through me, I saw the sin of them. Jesus Christ had died for this man; was I going to ask for more? Lord Jesus, I prayed, forgive me and help me to forgive him.*
>
> *I tried to smile, I struggled to raise my hand, but I could not. I felt nothing, not the slightest spark of warmth or charity. And so again I breathed a silent prayer. Jesus, I cannot forgive him. Give me your forgiveness.*
>
> *As I took his hand the most incredible thing happened. From my shoulder along my arm and through my hand a current seemed to pass from me to him, while into my heart sprang a love for this stranger that almost overwhelmed me.*
>
> *And so I discovered that it is not on our forgiveness any more than on our goodness that the world's healing hinges, but on his. When he tells us to love our enemies, he gives, along with the command, the love itself.*

FROM *THE HIDING PLACE*, CORRIE TEN BOOM

FOR REFLECTION

It is in pardoning that we are pardoned.

Travelling Companions

THE CHURCH

*When I was three or four, my eldest cousin came
to stay with our grandparents. I had never met him
before. He was seventeen, very tall and grown-up,
wearing a striped school blazer. I was immediately won
over when he produced from his pocket a bar of
chocolate he had brought for me. I put out my hand to
take it but my mother said I could not have it unless I
kissed him, to say thank you. I was far too much in
awe of him to do that. He might be one of the family,
but I still did not know him. For a long time I held out
and refused, but in the end my love of chocolate
prevailed and I agreed to the kiss. I soon lost my fear
and grew to love him as one of the close-knit family
circle that has played such an important part in my life
ever since.*

When we become Christians we are born into new life. We
share this life with every other person who has become God's
child. We become members of one huge family, with brothers
and sisters all over the world as well as down the ages.

The New Testament never thinks in terms of solitary
Christians but always of the community of God's people.
Different pictures are used to underline the unity that binds
Christians together. They are described as God's family, his
household, his chosen nation, his priests, his building, his
temple; Christ's body and Christ's bride.

All true followers of Jesus make up the church – which is
neither a denomination nor a building, but the total sum of

God's people. Paul's metaphor of the church as Christ's body helps us to see how closely we are linked with one another, whenever or wherever we live. We belong to one another as intimately as different organs of one body, connected and directed by Christ, the head.

Jesus wanted his people to be united and to love one another. He meant their love for one another to be the sign that they belonged to him. Sadly, it does not always happen. We need time to develop a close and loving relationship with other Christians and to feel at home in the life of the church family.

Relationships in human families are sometimes strained and so too within the church. What matters is that misunderstandings are put right, faults forgiven and love restored, so that we can move forward together.

We need other Christians. We need their friendship and support – the regular 'fellowship' which membership of a local church provides. Here we can worship together, pray together, listen to God's word, study the Bible together and encourage one another to live out our faith in daily life.

Other Christians need us as much as we need them. The Holy Spirit gives all of us gifts to use for the benefit of the Christian community. Whatever our differences of outlook or temperament, age or status, we can unite in our Christian work and worship, so that, with each playing their part, we grow steadily closer in love and mutual support on our journey together.

BIBLE SIGNPOSTS

Just as in a single human body there are many limbs and organs, all with different functions, so we who are united with Christ, though many, form one body, and belong to one another as its limbs and organs.... Let love of the Christian community show itself in mutual affection.

ROMANS 12:4-5, 10

We are all children of God through faith in Jesus Christ... We are no longer Jews or Greeks or slaves or free men or even merely men or women, but we are all the same – we are Christians; we are one in Christ Jesus.

GALATIANS 3:26, 28

You are no longer foreigners and aliens, but fellow-citizens with God's people and members of God's household, built on the foundation of the apostles and prophets, with Christ Jesus himself as the chief cornerstone... In him you too are being built together to become a dwelling in which God lives by his Spirit.

EPHESIANS 2:19-22

Those who accepted what Peter said were baptized...They met constantly to hear the apostles teach and to share the common life, to break bread, and to pray.

ACTS 2:41-42

Before Jesus returned to his Father, he left his disciples the task of spreading the good news of God's kingdom far and wide. He told them to baptize those who pledged themselves to follow him. Baptism was a familiar ceremony to Jewish people. Those who wanted to adopt the Jewish faith were baptized as a sign of initiation. John the Baptist baptized those who wanted to turn their lives around to God, as a sign of their change of heart and life.

Christian converts have also been baptized as Jesus taught, from earliest times. In baptism new Christians take their stand for Jesus, making public their personal act of faith. The apostle Paul described baptism as a symbolic act. Just as

Jesus died and rose again, so the Christian dies to the old life and rises again to new life in Jesus. For millions of Christians, baptism – or the Confirmation by which the vows of baptism are personally renewed – is a crucial step at the beginning of their pilgrimage.

Jesus also gave his disciples a special meal to share. Each year the Passover Festival was celebrated by the Jewish people, to commemorate God saving and rescuing his people from slavery in Egypt centuries before.

Just before his arrest and death, Jesus kept the Passover meal with his disciples. He transformed it into a celebration of the giving of his body and life-blood to save the world. Jesus told his followers to continue to take bread and wine in memory of him. Christians still celebrate that special meal, sharing bread and wine, to signify their oneness with Jesus, their Master, and with one another.

This service of Holy Communion – also called the Lord's Supper, the Eucharist or the Mass – is celebrated in many different ways and with different emphases. But for all Christians the sharing of the bread and wine in Holy Communion is a powerful and repeated means of renewal and enabling on the Christian journey.

TRAVELLERS' TALES

Now I saw in my dream, that Christian went not forth alone, for there was one whose name was Hopeful... who joined himself unto him, and entering into a brotherly covenant, told him that he would be his companion.

FROM *PILGRIM'S PROGRESS*, JOHN BUNYAN

Just as in our physical bodies every part contributes something important to the whole, so it is with our corporate body in Christ, the Church. Each of us should give way to his neighbour, according to the spiritual gifts the Lord has given him. The strong should not overlook the problems of their weaker brethren, and the weak should recognize the gifts of the strong. Wealthy Christians should share their riches with the poorer members, and those who benefit from their generosity should thank God for it.

CLEMENT OF ROME (30-100 AD)

This concept of the church as 'the people of God' – as God's new society, his family, his community – breaks upon many today as the most thrilling 'good news' they could ever hear. And what a transformation it can bring when a person knows that he belongs to God and to his people for ever! In an age of isolation, the joy of really belonging to God and being part of his people throughout the world – a belonging which depends not on earning acceptance, but on receiving freely of God's love – is one of the most relevant features of the Christian message of good news.

FROM I BELIEVE IN THE CHURCH, DAVID WATSON

The Church is the pilgrim people of God. It is on the move – hastening to the ends of the earth to beseech all men to be reconciled to God, and hastening to the end of time to meet its Lord who will gather all into one.

FROM THE HOUSEHOLD OF GOD, LESSLIE NEWBIGIN

Holy Communion is surely always falling short of its true purpose if it fails to produce some sense of solidarity with our fellow-worshippers... High and mysterious though it is, it is also the ordained place of deepest fellowship for those who are committed to the Way of Christ, ordinary, faulty, and imperfect though they are.

FROM APPOINTMENT WITH GOD, J.B. PHILLIPS

FOR REFLECTION

I'm not alone. My Christian brothers and sisters are travelling the same road.

On the Mountain Top

WORSHIP

When I was still very young my mother and an aunt took my sister and me to the Crystal Palace. It was a glittering dome of glass and iron created by Joseph Paxton for the Great Exhibition of 1851, later re-erected in south London. (I remember seeing the red sky from my bedroom window when, sadly, it burned to the ground in 1938.)

When evening fell we watched a firework display in the grounds of the Palace. I can remember standing on some stone steps, thrilled as I had never been before as each new explosion of light and colour lit up the sky. It was almost more than I could bear. I felt as if I would burst with the beauty and magnificence of it all. It seemed to me to be more than a mere spectacle – I felt myself to be part of all that loveliness and joy. I was caught up together with that huge crowd of people in an experience of wonder, splendour, excitement and shared delight.

To worship God means to recognize his worth and to own with gladness his right to have the supreme and unique place that only he is fit to occupy. We were created to find in God our source of joy and satisfaction and wonder, so it is not surprising that we find true fulfilment when we pour out our hearts and voices in worship to God.

But worship involves more than contemplating God and singing his praises, lifting up reverent and adoring hearts to him. The word 'worship', in the Greek of the New Testament, can also be translated 'service'. We worship God just as truly when we go about our daily life motivated by the desire to please and bring honour to him. Worship embraces every part of life. To worship God is to offer ourselves to him, body, mind and spirit. He is worth everything we can give and far, far more.

One of the joys of meeting with other Christians is that we can praise and worship God together. Shared worship lifts our hearts and minds, our wills and our emotions to a mountain-top experience which can seem like heaven begun.

BIBLE SIGNPOSTS

Shout for joy to the Lord, all the earth.
Worship the Lord with gladness;
come before him with joyful songs.
Know that the Lord is God.
It is he who made us, and we are his;
we are his people, the sheep of his pasture.
Enter his gates with thanksgiving
and his courts with praise;
give thanks to him and praise his name.
For the Lord is good and his love endures for ever;
his faithfulness continues through all generations.
PSALM 100

Fear the Lord your God, worship only him.
DEUTERONOMY 6:13

Jesus said: 'Those who worship God must worship in spirit and in truth.'
JOHN 4:23-24

My friends, I implore you by God's mercy to offer your very selves to him: a living sacrifice, dedicated and fit for his acceptance, the worship offered by mind and heart.
ROMANS 12:1

I heard all created things, in heaven, on earth, under the earth, and in the sea, crying: 'Praise and honour, glory and might, to him who sits on the throne and to the Lamb for ever!'

REVELATION 5:11-13

To worship God means to put him first. Everything else must take second place. In the Ten Commandments it is forbidden to 'bow down or worship' any other gods. These days our gods may not literally be images or idols; any thing or person that takes first place in our thoughts and desires is a substitute god.

People talk about looking after 'number one', and self-fulfilment and self-satisfaction easily become top priority. Many other things clamour for first place in life – not all of them bad by any means. But even good and legitimate interests cease to be so if they usurp God's place in our affection.

God is not an egotistical, authoritarian dictator who demands our complete devotion. He is a loving Creator who made us to be in family relationship with himself. He knows that we cannot find true peace and fulfilment until we return to God, our centre, and find our joy and rest in him. In the book of Revelation in the New Testament of the Bible, John's glimpse into heaven describes eternal happiness as the close presence of God and the freedom to worship and enjoy him for ever. That fulness of living can begin in wholehearted worship now.

TRAVELLERS' TALES

Worship is the submission of all our nature to God. It is... the most selfless emotion of which our nature is capable and therefore the chief remedy of that self-centredness which is our original sin and the source of all actual sin.

FROM *READINGS IN ST JOHN'S GOSPEL*, WILLIAM TEMPLE (1881-1944)

Joy Davidman, best known as the wife of C.S. Lewis, was Jewish by birth and a communist by belief before her conversion to Christianity. Here is what she says about the first commandment – to worship God alone:

What shape is an idol?

I worship Ganesa, brother, god of worldly wisdom, patron of shopkeepers.... I worship a Rolls Royce sports model, brother. All my days I give it offerings of oil and polish... I worship my house beautiful, sister. Long and loving meditation have I spent on it... What shape is your idol, sister? Is it your house, or your clothes, or perhaps even your worthwhile and cultural club?

I worship the pictures I paint, brother... I worship my job;... I worship my golf game, my bridge game... I worship my comfort; after all, isn't enjoyment the goal of life?... I worship my church... I worship myself...

What shape is your idol?...

Does it matter which of our toys we make into a god? What matters is that the thing is still a toy, an idol – a material object on which we rely to bring us happiness... Why should I prefer to worship a small and limited idol, rather than a great and universal God? Perhaps because I can own the idol, whereas no man can own God, whose justice is incorruptible.

FROM SMOKE ON THE MOUNTAIN, JOY DAVIDMAN

O Lord, you are great, you are to be highly praised;
Your power is great
and there are no limits to your wisdom.
And man, a tiny part
of your creative work,
wants to celebrate your praise,
man, who drags his own frailty behind him,
as a testimony to his sin
and to your desire to reject the proud;
in spite of this

a small part of your great work of creation
wants to celebrate your praise.
It is you who have aroused this desire in us
because you made us for yourself,
and our hearts will not be at peace
until they rest in you

FROM CONFESSIONS, AUGUSTINE OF HIPPO (354-430)

Isaac Penington, the son of a distinguished Puritan, renounced his wealth to join the new Society of Friends – the Quakers. He spent eleven years in prison for his beliefs. His writings, published after his death, describe Quaker worship:

Our worship is a deep exercise of our spirits before the Lord... and we pray in the spirit, and with the new understanding, as God pleaseth to quicken, draw forth, and open our hearts towards himself.

Cheer the Lord, everyone!
Everything, praise him!
Cheer him from our skies;
praise him from outer space...
Cheer him, sun and moon;
praise him all distant galaxies.
Cheer him, all who are close to his heart;
praise him all mysteries beyond our knowledge.
All of you, cheer the Lord,
for he speaks and you come into being.
He gives you a place for ever;
He fixes the universal laws...

Prime ministers and presidents of the earth;
cabinet ministers and high court judges;
Exuberant teenagers,
old people and children,
Come on, all of you, cheer the Lord;

he alone is worth it!
His glory transfigures this earth,
and blazes from a million suns.
He has given mankind high honour;
heroes will applaud his faithfulness.
Those who trust his presence will shout:
'Cheer the Lord!'

PSALM 148, BRUCE D. PREWER, *AUSTRALIAN PSALMS*

FOR REFLECTION

We were created 'to glorify God and to enjoy him for ever'.

Dressed for the Journey

LIFESTYLE

Before I was old enough to go to school I would wait for my mother in the early afternoon at the foot of the stairs. She would always go to her room to change after lunch, taking off her morning clothes and putting on something suitable for any visitors who might call. When she came down the stairs, smiling at me, I thought her the most beautiful person in the world. I still remember two of the dresses that she used to wear. One was a deep rose crêpe de Chine. (I was greatly upset when she had it dyed black for my grandmother's funeral.) The other was of bottle-green satin, with a fan-shaped bow over one shoulder. I loved those dresses and I loved my mother. The clothes seemed to fit and become her perfectly.

In the early days of the church, as today, baptism signified a determination to be done with the old life and to begin a new life – and a new lifestyle – as a Christian. To symbolize this change, those being baptized took off their old clothes before baptism. Afterwards they dressed in clean white garments.

Paul uses the picture of clothes when he writes about our new look as Christians. He reminds his readers that they can never be good enough for God in their own right. But Jesus dresses us in his goodness. This covers our own failings and imperfections. When God looks at us he sees us dressed in the clean clothes of Jesus' righteousness.

BIBLE SIGNPOSTS

What you learned was to fling off the dirty clothes of the old way of living... and, with yourselves mentally and spiritually re-

*made, to put on the clean fresh clothes of the new life which
was made by God's design.*
EPHESIANS 4:22-24

*Christ was without sin, but for our sake God made him share
our sin in order that in union with him we might share the
righteousness of God.*
2 CORINTHIANS 5:21

*By God's act you are in Christ Jesus; God has made him our
wisdom, and in him we have our righteousness, our holiness,
our liberation.*
1 CORINTHIANS 1:30

*I now have the righteousness that is given through faith in Christ,
the righteousness that comes from God and is based on faith.*
PHILIPPIANS 3:9

*Clothe yourselves with the Lord Jesus Christ, and do not think
about how to gratify the desires of the sinful nature.*
ROMANS 13:14

In the New Testament of the Bible the apostle Paul reminds us
that we must do our part to 'put on clean clothes'. We are to
take action in order to live the new style of life that will please
God. Off must come the dirty old rags of greed, lust,
dishonesty, temper, foul language and unkind gossip. On must
go the clean clothes of kindness, generosity, helpful talk and
loving, understanding attitudes.

But Paul recognizes that we can't make that
transformation by ourselves. Jesus' Spirit, who lives in us, will
gently help us to grow more like Jesus, if we let him. His aim is
for the new clothes gradually to become part of us, to suit us
and fit us and make us beautiful for God.

TRAVELLERS' TALES

Origen lived in Alexandria from about 185 to 254 AD. He was

an outstanding theologian and writer, who was later tortured for his faith:

> There would be no need for the Holy Spirit if we could become holy in our own strength, but God has sent him to be our aid because we can't...
>
> It is when the Holy Spirit has worked in us, making holy what was before unclean, that we can go on to receive God's righteousness in Christ. That is to say, it is not our holiness, but his, given to us through the power of the Spirit as he works in us...
>
> So the believer is intended to make progress, to grow. The Father gives natural life to everybody, but his purpose for us is so much more than that. He wishes us to go on to share more and more fully in Christ's righteousness, understanding and wisdom. Eventually – as the Holy Spirit cleanses and purifies us – all the stains of human sin and ignorance are removed and the being made by God becomes worthy of God.
>
> ORIGEN (C.185 – C.254 AD)

In 1373 Dame Julian of Norwich received sixteen revelations of the love of God, which were later written down. She became an anchoress (hermit) and meditated on the revelations she had received. She seems also to have given counsel and spiritual help to those who came to her:

> Our Lord showed me spiritually how intimately he loves us... He does not despise the work of his hands... He loves the soul he has made in his own likeness. For just as the body is clothed in its garments, and the flesh in its skin, and the bones in their flesh, and the heart in its body, so too are we, soul and body, clothed head and foot in the goodness of God. Yes, and even more closely than that, for all these things will decay and wear out, whereas the goodness of God is unchanging.
>
> FROM REVELATIONS, JULIAN OF NORWICH (B.1342)

The New Testament... talks about Christians being 'born again';

it talks about them 'putting on Christ'; about Christ 'being formed in us'; about our coming to 'have the mind of Christ'.

Put right out of your head the idea that these are only fancy ways of saying that Christians are to read what Christ said and try to carry it out... They mean something much more than that. They mean that a real Person, Christ, here and now, in that very room where you're saying your prayers, is doing things to you... killing the old natural self in you and replacing it with the kind of self he has. At first, only for moments. Then for longer periods... Of course, it is God who does everything. We, at most, allow it to be done to us.

FROM *BEYOND PERSONALITY*, C.S. LEWIS

Malcolm Muggeridge, twentieth-century wit and man of letters, was first drawn to Christ through meeting Mother Teresa. Early one morning, he saw her off on a train from Calcutta:

When the train began to move, and I walked away, I felt as though I were leaving behind me all the beauty and all the joy of the universe. Something of God's universal love has rubbed off on Mother Teresa, giving her homely features a notable luminosity; a shining quality. She has lived so closely with her Lord that the same enchantment clings about her that sent the crowds chasing after him in Jerusalem and Galilee, and made his mere presence seem a harbinger of healing.

FROM *SOMETHING BEAUTIFUL FOR GOD*, MALCOLM MUGGERIDGE

Spirit of grace,
Reveal in me my Saviour,
That I may gaze upon his mirrored face,
Till I reflect it in my whole behaviour.

RICHARD WILTON (1827-1903)

FOR REFLECTION

God clothes me with Christ's goodness.

Reaching the Heartland

LOVE

My sister and I were very excited when a family of three cousins came for a holiday to my grandparents. They were much older than me – two boys and a girl – and the girl was in a wheelchair.

But what fun we had together. The two boys would sometimes race their sister's wheelchair – with her in it! Whenever there was something interesting to do or see, one of them would rush to fetch her and push her to the scene of the action. It was not a chore to them because their enjoyment came from doing things together. I was not left out either, although I was so young. With a little prompting, my patient girl cousin made up endless adventure stories to tell me, about a fictional 'Billy-Boy'. Our happiness and shared experiences sprang from their love for one another which spread out spontaneously to include us too.

We begin to understand what love is really like when we see how God loves us. His love spreads out to include us all. God's love led him to give himself, in the person of Jesus, to rescue a world that had turned its back on him. God's love actually reaches out to those who are his enemies.

There is all the difference in the world between acts of duty and acts of love. It is possible to receive necessary attention and help but to recognize that it is given grudgingly or out of a sense of what has to be done. God's love is never like that. He loves us with unbounded warmth and generosity. His love is unconditional and freely given.

BIBLE SIGNPOSTS

God said, 'I have dearly loved you from of old, and still I maintain my unfailing care for you.'

JEREMIAH 31:3

This is how God showed his love among us: he sent his one and only Son into the world that we might live through him. This is love: not that we loved God, but that he loved us and sent his Son as an atoning sacrifice for our sins. Dear friends, since God so loved us, we also ought to love one another. No one has ever seen God; but if we love one another, God lives in us and his love is made complete in us.

1 JOHN 4:7-12

'Teacher, which is the greatest commandment in the law?' Jesus answered: '"Love the Lord your God with all your heart, with all your soul, and with all your mind." That is the greatest, the first commandment. The second is like it: "Love your neighbour as yourself." Everything in the law and the prophets hang on these two commandments.'

MATTHEW 22:36-40

Jesus said: 'I give you a new commandment: love one another; as I have loved you, so you are to love one another. If there is this love among you, then everyone will know that you are my disciples.'

JOHN 13:34-35

Love is patient and kind. Love envies no one, is never boastful, never conceited, never rude; love is never selfish, never quick to take offence. Love keeps no score of wrongs, takes no pleasure in the sins of others, but delights in the truth. There is nothing love cannot face; there is no limit to its faith, its hope, its endurance.

1 CORINTHIANS 13:4-7

Love is probably the most misunderstood word in the English language. It is often used to mean sexual attraction. The same word describes deep liking or affection between family and friends or the magnet that attracts us to kindred spirits. It nearly always defines feelings and people often conclude that when feelings fade or change, love no longer survives and the relationship should be broken off.

Christian love is concerned less with feelings and more with attitudes and intentions. Love wants the very best for others. It is not a cold, charitable 'do-gooding' but a sensitive understanding and meeting of another's deepest needs. It does not spoil or indulge and can sometimes be tough, but it always works towards the other's best interests. This may sound too good to be true and we often fall short of putting such love into practice. But genuine, mutual concern for one another transforms individuals and groups of people and gives a little taste of what God's love is like.

If we are to show this kind of love consistently we need to keep on receiving fresh supplies of God's love at the deepest level of our being. Receiving God's love and responding to him in love leads to loving other people too and giving ourselves wholeheartedly and willingly for them.

TRAVELLERS' TALES

The love of God Most High for our soul is so wonderful that it surpasses all knowledge. No created being can know the greatness, the sweetness, the tenderness of the love that our Maker has for us... For love he made mankind, and out of the same love he willed to become man... Love makes might and wisdom come down to our level... I saw in Christ what the Father is like.

FROM *REVELATIONS*, JULIAN OF NORWICH (B.1342)

The Rt Rev. Festo Kivengere, evangelist, teacher and writer, was an outstanding bishop in Uganda. He narrowly escaped death at the hands of Idi Amin. Yet one of his books has the title *I Love Idi Amin*. He writes here about a day when he had hurt his wife's feelings. With God's help, he asks Mera's forgiveness and eventually harmony is restored.

> *In the atmosphere of mutual forgiveness, and in the provision that Jesus Christ has made for us, Mera and I have discovered that through self-forgetting and self-sacrificing is born a truly creative love. Instead of one emptying the other person for one's own need, each fulfils the other, making him or her more of a person, having more dignity. It brings out the latent qualities in the other, and it partakes somewhat of the love of Christ.*
>
> FROM *REVOLUTIONARY LOVE*, FESTO KIVENGERE (1920-88)

Amy Carmichael, born in Ireland in 1867, went as a missionary to India where she founded the Dohnavur Fellowship, a home which rescued and cared for children given to the temples to become cult prostitutes. For nearly twenty years, following an accident, Amy Carmichael was housebound, but she continued to influence many through her prayers and her writings.

> *In Tamil we have a polite word, which tells someone who asks for something that we have nothing to give; we have run short of it – Poochiam.*
>
> *One day I felt like saying Poochiam about love, I had run short of it. I was in the Forest, and I had just read a letter that was hard to answer lovingly. I was sitting by The Pool at the time, and presently began to watch the water flow down through the deep channel worn in the smooth rocks above it. There was always inflow, so there was always outflow. Never for one minute did the water cease to flow in, and so never for one moment did it cease to flow out; and I knew, of course, that the water that flowed out was the water that flowed in. The hollow that*

we called The Pool had no water of its own, and yet all
the year round there was an overflow.

God hath not given you the Spirit of fear... but of
love.

If love flows in, love will flow out. Let love flow
in. That was the word of The Pool. There is no need for
any of us to run short of love. We need never say
Poochiam.

FROM *EDGES OF HIS WAYS*, AMY CARMICHAEL

Gordon Wilson became widely known overnight in 1987, when
his daughter was killed by an IRA bomb at a Remembrance
Day service in Enniskillen, Northern Ireland. His integrity,
forgiveness and Christian love made a deep impression on all
who heard his words, which were broadcast just after the
accident.

The wall collapsed... and we were thrown forward...
rubble and stones... all around us and under us. I
remember thinking... 'I'm not hurt'... but there's a pain in
my shoulder... I shouted to Marie, 'Are you all right?' and
she said, 'Yes'... She found my hand and said, 'Is that your
hand, Dad?...' I said, 'Are you all right, dear?'... but we
were under six feet of rubble... three or four times I asked
her... she always said, 'Yes, I'm all right'... I asked her the
fifth time... 'Are you all right, Marie?'... She said, 'Daddy,
I love you very much...' Those were the last words she
spoke to me... I kept shouting, 'Marie, are you all right?'...
There was no reply.

I have lost my daughter, but I bear no ill will, I bear
no grudge... Dirty sort of talk is not going to bring her
back to life... I don't have an answer... But I know there
has to be a plan. If I didn't think that I would commit
suicide... It's part of a greater plan, and God is good... and
we shall meet again.

FROM *MARIE*, GORDON WILSON

My Lord is the source of Love; I the river's course.
Let God's love flow through me. I will not obstruct it.
Irrigation ditches can water but a portion of the field;
the great Yangtze River can water a thousand acres.
Expand my heart, O Lord, that I may love yet more
   people.
The waters of love can cover vast tracts,
nothing will be lost to me.
The greater the outward flow, the greater the returning
   tide.
If I am not linked to Love's source, I will dry up.
If I dam the waters of Love, they will stagnate.
Can I compare my heart with the boundless seas?
But abandon not the measure of my heart, O Lord.
Let the waves of your love still billow there!

'LILIES OF THE FIELD', WANG WEIFAN

FOR REFLECTION

Where there is hatred, let me bring your love.

The Constant Guide

GOD'S PRESENCE

When I was very young only the well-off owned cars and we were not well-off. But a middle-aged couple with a large green limousine and no children of their own used to take us out from time to time. My great joy was to sit in front with Mr Butcher (my mother and sister and talkative Mrs Butcher keeping up a constant hum of conversation in the back) as we glided smoothly through lanes and towns. Most of the time I chattered to him, confiding my hopes and interests, content to watch his capable hands on the wheel and see his placid smile as he listened to me. Often I would pester to know where we were going but he always kept it a surprise. Once it was the seaside, another time a warm inland lake, where we paddled before having tea in a restaurant – a treat in itself. But it was my unlikely companionship with Mr Butcher and the pleasure of his company that gave warmth and enjoyment to those far-off summer afternoons.

It sometimes seems as if the Bible gives us two different pictures of God. He is portrayed as great and mighty, powerful and far beyond our reach – transcendent. But he is also described as 'immanent' – close to us, concerned with our affairs and involved in our lives. Some think that the Old Testament lays stress on the distant, just and all-powerful God and the New Testament highlights the God who is close, gentle and forgiving. But that does not fit the facts. The Old Testament clearly describes God as loving and forgiving his people – comparing him with a tender father or faithful husband to them. The New Testament writers speak plainly about God's love but also about his awesomeness and majesty. If we are to get a true picture of what God is like we must accept both definitions. God is holy and righteous: all sin is alien to his nature. His power and goodness are far above and beyond what we can imagine. But he is also ready and waiting to come close to us in a loving family relationship.

THE TRINITY

Christians describe God as a Trinity – three persons in one. At first sight that seems to add to the complications. But it can actually help us to understand more about God.

Christians believe in one God, but the Bible describes him in three ways – as God the Father, as Jesus the Son, and as God the Holy Spirit. In some way, too mysterious for us to understand, we must accept that God is a unity, yet he makes himself known to us as three persons. St Patrick likened the Trinity to the shamrock. It is a single leaf, but has three separate parts to it. Nothing, of course, can give a complete picture of God because he is beyond human understanding. But we can hold on to the insights that the Trinity makes clearer for us.

The unity of the three in one tells us that God is not a solitary Being but a God of harmony and loving relationships. Within the Trinity there is perfect unity and love.

The Trinity can also help us understand the different ways in which God relates to our world. God the Son has taken on our nature and came among us as a perfect human being. He showed us what God is like by the way he lived and what he said and did. He could claim: 'Anyone who has seen me has seen the Father.' He was able to rescue us from the bitter results of human sin because he was both perfect man and also God. He broke the stranglehold of sin and death by experiencing death and bearing the inevitable judgement of sin on our behalf. When he rose from death he demonstrated his victory over the powers of evil, bringing us new life and victory too.

Jesus was on earth for only a short time. But he told his followers that he would send another Helper to them – his Holy Spirit, sometimes called the Spirit of Jesus. In Old Testament times, God's Holy Spirit is described as coming occasionally upon an individual, such as a king or leader, to help them do some special task for God. But on the Jewish Feast of Pentecost – six weeks after Jesus' return to his Father, when Jerusalem was packed with pilgrims – Jesus' promise came true. The Holy Spirit came to all the Christian disciples irrespective of sex, status or age and completely changed them. Before, they had been frightened and confused but the Holy Spirit gave them courage and power to tell the crowds what God had done through Jesus. From that day to this, God's Holy Spirit has come to live within every true believer and follower of Jesus. So God is always with us, close and real, making his home within us and also within the community of the church.

Jesus described the Holy Spirit of God in many ways. He called him the Helper, the Strengthener, the Advocate (the one who pleads our cause) and the Spirit of Truth, who teaches us the truth about Jesus.

But it is important not to be too cut and dried in the way we split up and divide the work of the Trinity. The first verses of the Bible tells us that when God the Father made the world the Spirit of God was in action too, bringing order out of chaos. And in the Gospel of John we read that without Jesus 'no created thing came into being'. So all the persons of the Trinity were at work in the creation of our world.

The three-in-one God is also involved in our salvation. Jesus was not acting alone to bring us to God. God the Father was at one with Jesus, bringing us back to himself. The Spirit too is at work, for Jesus described those who come into his kingdom as being 'born of the Spirit'.

When we pray, Jesus told us to say 'Our Father', but we are

to ask in Jesus' name. We are also told that the Holy Spirit helps and directs our prayers. So it is the three-in-one God who is involved in our creation, salvation, and daily Christian experience.

BIBLE SIGNPOSTS

Jesus said: 'If you really love me, you will keep the commandments I have given you and I shall ask the Father to give you someone else to stand by you, to be with you always. I mean the Spirit of truth, whom the world cannot accept, for it can neither see nor recognize that Spirit. But you recognize him, for he is with you now and will be in your hearts.'
JOHN 14:15-17

Jesus said: 'I will be with you always, to the end of time.'
MATTHEW 28:20

God has said, 'I will never leave you or desert you.' So we can take courage and say, 'The Lord is my helper, I will not fear; what can man do to me?'
HEBREWS 13:5-6

Do not make God's Holy Spirit sad.
EPHESIANS 4:30

Never damp the fire of the Spirit.
1 THESSALONIANS 5:19

Let the Holy Spirit fill you.
EPHESIANS 5:18

The grace of the Lord Jesus Christ, and the love of God, and the fellowship of the Holy Spirit, be with you all.
2 CORINTHIANS 13:14

When Jesus promised to be with his disciples always, he kept that promise in the coming of the Holy Spirit. He is God with us, now as then, in the closest and most real sense. But it is possible for us to neglect him or overlook his presence. We can forget that he is with us.

It is also possible to make the Holy Spirit sad by our disobedience to God or to stifle his power and influence within us by asserting our own self-will. Instead we should actively and deliberately recognize his presence. We should talk to him and listen to his voice; then he will prompt our words and actions. Some Christians describe this conscious communing with God's Spirit as 'practising the presence of God'. We do this when we recognize his closeness and involvement in all we do and deliberately bring him into our decision-making and our actions.

As well as constantly recognizing God's closeness, we can devote brief times in our busy lives for quietness and communion with God. Meditation for a Christian is not the repeating of mantras but the deliberate opening up of our thoughts and feelings to the God who is with us. When we are quiet we can listen to his voice, which prompts us to go God's way. As we open up to him we can also allow his peace and strength to flow in and fill our lives. Christians down the ages have discovered and described for us different ways in which we can enjoy God as constant Guide and Companion on the journey of the Spirit. The Christ within also prompts love and compassion for the Christ in others.

TRAVELLERS' TALES

Brother Lawrence became a lay brother with a Carmelite order in Paris in 1666. He made it his aim, whether in the kitchens or on an uncomfortable trip overseas, to buy wine for the brothers; to 'walk as in God's presence'. M. Beaufort, who collected Brother Lawrence's words and letters, describes this:

As he proceeded in his work he continued his familiar

*conversation with his Maker, imploring his grace, and
offering to him all his actions...*

*'Thus,' said he, 'by rising after my falls, and by
frequently renewed acts of faith and love, I am come to a
state where it would be as difficult for me not to think of
God as it was at first to accustom myself to it.'*

*It was observed that in the greatest hurry of business
in the kitchen he still preserved his recollection and
heavenly-mindedness. He was never hasty nor loitering,
but did each thing in its season, with an even,
uninterrupted composure and tranquillity of spirit. 'The
time of business,' said he, 'does not with me differ from the
time of prayer; and in the noise and clatter of my kitchen,
while several persons are at the same time calling for
different things, I possess God in as great tranquillity as if
I were upon my knees at the blessed sacrament.'*

FROM *THE PRACTICE OF THE PRESENCE OF GOD*

*I often used to visit, on church business, an old pastor who
never let me go without praying with me. He would
address his prayers to Jesus, and I was struck one day by
his extreme simplicity. It was as if he were continuing
aloud an intimate conversation that he was always
carrying on with him.*

*When I got back home I talked it over with my wife,
and together we asked God to give us also the close
fellowship with Jesus that that old pastor had. Since then
he has been the centre of my devotion and my travelling
companion. He takes pleasure in what I do and concerns
himself with it. He is a friend with whom I can discuss
everything that happens in my life. He shares my joy and
my pain, my hopes and fears... Jesus Christ does not take
our humanity from us; he comes down into it, so that I
can bring my difficulties and failures to him, and that also
helps to maintain our fellowship.*

FROM *A DOCTOR'S CASEBOOK IN THE LIGHT OF THE BIBLE*, PAUL TOURNIER
(20TH-CENTURY SWISS PHYSICIAN AND WRITER)

Remember God more often than you breathe.
GREGORY OF NAZIANZUS (DIED 389)

How shall I pray to God – my God, my Lord? It seems strange to ask him to 'come into my heart'. After all, he is the God who made the heavens and the earth, and the Bible tells me that even they cannot contain him. So how can my poor, small heart invite him in?...

I can pray truly that my heart, where you already have a foothold, may receive more and more of you, until one day the whole of me will be filled with the whole of you.
AUGUSTINE OF HIPPO (354-430)

The essence of prayer is to hear the voice of another, of Christ, but likewise to hear the voice of each person I meet in whom Christ addresses me. His voice comes to me in every human voice, and his face is infinitely varied... God became incarnate so that man might contemplate his face in every face. Perfect prayer seeks this presence of Christ and recognizes it in every human face.
FROM *POUSTINIA*, CATHERINE DE HUECK

Dearest Lord, may I see you today and every day in the person of your sick, and, whilst nursing them, minister unto you.
MOTHER TERESA OF CALCUTTA

God, our Companion on the journey,
let us not be so caught up in worldly cares
that we forget that you are with us everywhere.
Open our eyes that we may meet you
in the people squashed against us in the crowded bus,
in the weary shoppers elbowing their way towards the
counter,
in the sightseers sauntering along the pavements,
in the beggars squatting in their squalid corners,
in the noisy children kicking around an old tin can,

and in the lonely pensioner peering out of a grimy window.
O God, our Companion,
let us never forget that you are with us everywhere.

JEAN GASKIN

Your supporting presence guides us through the night
So we can approach you, sparkling Source of light;
Shine through the mists, the deadening heavy clay.
Purifying Spirit, burn the dross away.

You are gentler weather after winter's rains,
And a wayside restplace soothing journeying's strains;
Though out in front, protect us with yourself:
You're our destination and the road itself.

JUNE BOYCE-TILLMAN (BASED ON ALFRED'S TRANSLATION OF BOETHIUS)

FOR REFLECTION

The Maker of heaven and earth stoops to live in the heart of every one of his children.

In Touch with Home

PRAYER

Although we no longer lived with our grandparents, we still spent our summer holidays with them at the seaside. Breakfast over, it might be thought that we headed straight for the beach. But first came family prayers. I used to kneel beside my chair, the faint smell of the cushion assailing my nose, longing for the 'Amen' that would signal the end – and our freedom! But a long time had to elapse before I heard that welcome word. My grandfather, at prayer, was oblivious of everything – even the harsh chimes of the kitchen clock – as he worshipped, praised and petitioned his God. I sensed then that he was in another world. But it would be many years before I found that world for myself.

Isaiah, the Old Testament prophet, had a vision of God which left an indelible impression. At the beginning of his life-work he saw God, high and enthroned, his majestic presence filling every corner of the magnificent temple. Heavenly beings attended him, their faces shielded from the brightness of his glory, calling 'Holy, holy, holy!' The building shook and clouds of smoke began to fill the room. Isaiah was overpowered by the greatness and majesty of God. More than that, he experienced a deep sense of his own unworthiness in the light of God's purity and 'otherness'. God is not simply 'one of us' on a larger and more powerful scale. He is holy, distinct from us and different, beyond our imagining.

What Isaiah saw remains true. But Jesus brings us close to

God. He encourages us to think of him as 'Father'. The Holy
Spirit helps us pray and interprets our hesitating desires and
thoughts to God. But although we enjoy such intimacy and
closeness, we must never forget that when we pray we are in
the presence of a great and all-powerful God. He made us, our
world, and the vast universe we wonder at. We are only able to
come close to him because he is also full of love and forgiving
kindness.

BIBLE SIGNPOSTS

*God is in heaven and you are on earth, so let your words
be few.*
ECCLESIASTES 5:2

*Jesus said: 'When you pray, go into a room by yourself,
shut the door and pray to your Father who is in secret...
Do not go babbling on like the heathen, who imagine that
the more they say the more likely they are to be heard. Do
not imitate them, for your Father knows what your needs
are before you ask him. This is how you should pray:*
    *Our Father in heaven, may your name be hallowed;
your kingdom come, your will be done, on earth as in
heaven. Give us today our daily bread. Forgive us the
wrongs we have done, as we have forgiven those who have
wronged us. And do not put us to the test, but save us
from the evil one.'*
MATTHEW 6:6-13

*Don't worry over anything whatever; tell God every detail
of your needs in earnest and thankful prayer, and the
peace of God, which transcends human understanding,
will keep constant guard over your hearts and minds as
they rest in Christ Jesus.*
PHILIPPIANS 4:6-7

Practising God's presence means communing with God and recognizing his Holy Spirit's closeness to us at any time of the day or night. But Christians find that they also need to set aside times specifically for prayer. Many do this at the beginning and end of the day. We need times when we can block off other thoughts and activities and come to God – if possible without interruption. Regular prayer of this kind is much easier at some stages of life than at others; God understands our particular circumstances and does not lay down rules and regulations.

Our prayer will include different ingredients – as shown in the Lord's Prayer, the pattern for our prayers. We shall want to worship and praise God for his wonder and greatness and thank him for all the good things he gives to us. We will confess our failure and wrongdoing – specifically – not only in a general way. We will also share with him our needs and those of our loved ones, and we will pray for the wider needs of the world and for the working out of God's purposes.

Prayer is not a one-way conversation. If we are quiet in God's presence he will help us to see life from his perspective and learn to fit in with his plans for us (rather than pressure him to agree to ours!). Prayer is not a matter of persuading God to give us what we want, but of putting ourselves in his hands and learning to do things his way. As we listen in prayer, we give God a chance to prompt us to action or quieten us to wait patiently.

Sometimes God answers our prayers in a wonderful way. But there are also times when God seems to turn a deaf ear to our requests. Sometimes God does not rescue us from difficulties when we ask him to because he wants us to learn to handle them with his help. This is one way in which we can become stronger people and learn to trust God more. At other times God answers our prayers as a wise father. Like every good parent, he does not give us everything we ask for, only what is for our own and others' good. God's greatest desire is to help us become more like Jesus.

There will still be times when we cannot understand why God seems to ignore our prayers. This can be specially hard when we are praying for someone we love. We cannot always work out the reason, but we can be certain that God does hear and care. Jesus told us that we 'should always pray, and never become discouraged'. Recognizing that God knows the full story and loves those we care about even more than we do, helps us to go on trusting him, whether we understand what he is doing or not.

Prayer is not just a solitary or private experience. Jesus promised that when two people agree on a matter and pray together about it, God will hear and answer. Friends and families, husbands and wives, have found that God keeps that promise. The church family needs to pray together too. We are brought closer to one another as we worship God, tell him about the needs and concerns we share and ask his Spirit to guide us.

There are many traditions of prayer and many forms of prayer that we can use. But no special formula or language is needed in order to make God hear. Often we will want to talk to God using our own words. At other times prayers written for us by understanding and experienced Christians down the ages express what we want to say better than our own words can. Sometimes prayer will be silent, as we lift our hearts and thoughts to God without words. What matters is that we take time to pray, and that we come to God simply and honestly.

TRAVELLERS' TALES

Madame Guyon was a French aristocrat, born in 1648, who was persecuted for her religious beliefs. She practised Quietism, a devotion to prayer and stillness:

> Do not turn to prayer hoping to enjoy spiritual
> delights; rather come to prayer totally content to

receive nothing or to receive great blessing from God's
hand, which ever should be your heavenly Father's
will for you at that time. This will enable you to live
close to God in times of sadness as well as in times
when you are being comforted by God. It will also
prevent you from being surprised when you go through
times of spiritual aridity or when you feel as if you are
rejected by God.

FROM A SHORT AND EASY METHOD OF PRAYER

A person who prays is one who can once more breathe
freely, who has the freedom to move where he wishes,
with no fears to haunt him.

FROM WITH OPEN HANDS, HENRI NOUWEN

John Donne, a seventeenth-century wit and poet, repented the
ardent love poetry of his youth and turned to religious verse.
He became Dean of St Paul's Cathedral where crowds flocked
to hear him preach.

When we consider... the manifold weaknesses of the
strongest devotions in time of prayer, it is a sad
consideration. I throw myself down in my chamber, and
I call in and invite God and his angels thither, and
when they are there, I neglect God and his angels for
the noise of a fly, for the rattling of a coach, for the
whining of a door; I talk on, in the same posture of
praying – eyes lifted up – knees bowed down – as
though I prayed to God; and if God, or his angels,
should ask me when I last thought of God in that
prayer, I cannot tell. Sometimes I find that I had forgot
what I was about, but when I began to forget it, I
cannot tell. A memory of yesterday's pleasures, a fear
of tomorrow's dangers, a straw under my knee, a noise
in my ear, a light in my eye, an anything, a nothing, a
fancy, a chimera in my brain, troubles me in prayer. So

*certainly is there nothing, nothing in spiritual things,
perfect in this world.*

FROM THE SERMONS OF JOHN DONNE (?1572-1631)

Dag Hammarskjöld was a Swedish statesman who became
Secretary General of the United Nations. He was a brilliant
and skilled negotiator. It was while he was working to solve the
crisis in the Congo in 1961 that he was tragically killed in an
aircrash. He was posthumously awarded the Nobel peace prize.

Markings – his personal journal – was published after his
death. In his own words: 'These notes? They were sign-posts...
a fixed point which was on no account to be lost sight of'.

*Hallowed be thy name
        not mine,
Thy kingdom come,
        not mine,
Thy will be done,
        not mine,
Give us peace with thee
    Peace with men
    Peace with ourselves,
And free us from all fear*

FROM *MARKINGS*, DAG HAMMARSKJÖLD (1905-61)

*Those who approach the Lord should make their prayers
in a state of quietness, of peace and great tranquillity
without uneasy and confused cries but by applying their
attention to the Lord by the effort of the heart and the
soberness of their thoughts.*

SIXTH HOMILY FROM PSEUDO-MACARIUS (4TH/5TH CENTURY)

*Prayer is the most important thing in my life. If I should
neglect it for a single day, I should lose a great deal of the
fire of faith.*

MARTIN LUTHER (1483-1546)

To be there before you, Lord, that's all.
To shut the eyes of my body,
To shut the eyes of my soul,
And to be still and silent,
To expose myself to you who are there, exposed to me.
To be there before you, the Eternal Presence.
I am willing to feel nothing, Lord,
             to see nothing
    to hear nothing,
Empty of all ideas,
             of all images,
In the darkness.
Here I am, simply
To meet you without obstacles,
In the silence of faith,
Before you, Lord.

FROM *PRAYERS OF LIFE*, MICHEL QUOIST

We beseech you, O Lord our God,
be patient with us sinners.
You who know our weakness,
protect the work of your hands
now and in times to come,
deliver us from all temptation
and all danger
and from the powers of darkness of this world,
and bring us
into the kingdom of your only Son and our God.
For to your most holy Name
be the glory,
Father, Son and Holy Spirit,
now and for ever,
to the ages of ages. Amen.

PRAYER OF THE ORTHODOX CHURCH

FOR REFLECTION

Almighty God uses the prayers of his children to bring about his good purposes.

Light on the Path

THE BIBLE

One summer evening long after bedtime, my father took my sister and me out of doors. He wanted to show us something very special. We stood stock still, amazed by the lightness around us. The whole sky was illuminated with a soft sheet of yellow light. My father explained that this was the Northern Lights – the Aurora Borealis. The name sounded as beautiful as the sight. I looked at the houses around and could see them clearly. The darkness was banished; everything was bathed in a gentle and transforming light.

The Bible psalmist described God's words as 'a lamp to my feet and a light on my path'. The Bible is one of the chief ways in which God has spoken to us and down the ages Christians have found that it sheds light on their lives.

When Jesus was tempted to waver from God's plan for his life, he called to mind words from the Bible. He repeatedly said: 'It is written...' in order to direct the light of God's word onto his decision-making. As a Jewish boy his education centred on study of the Jewish Scriptures – the Old Testament in the Christian Bible. They became part of his thinking, understanding and wisdom, as the Bible has been for generations of men and women down the centuries.

There is nothing magic about the words of Scripture and mere knowledge of the Bible will not automatically change attitudes and actions. But when it is thoughtfully read and understood and when the reader intends, through prayer and the help of the Holy Spirit, to put its teaching into practice, the influence of the Bible is life-changing. The Bible is called God's Word because God speaks to us through what it has to say.

BIBLE SIGNPOSTS

The law of the Lord is perfect and revives the soul.
The Lord's instruction never fails;
it makes the simple wise.
The precepts of the Lord are right
and give joy to the heart.
The commandment of the Lord is pure
and gives light to the eyes.
The fear of the Lord is unsullied; it abides for ever.
The Lord's judgements are true and righteous every one,
more to be desired than gold, pure gold in plenty,
sweeter than honey dripping from the comb.
It is through them that your servant is warned;
in obeying them is great reward.
PSALM 19:7-11

The Holy Scriptures... are able to give you the wisdom
that leads to salvation through faith in Christ Jesus. All
Scripture is inspired by God and is useful for teaching the
truth, rebuking error, correcting faults, and giving
instruction for right living, so that the person who serves
God may be fully qualified and equipped to do every kind
of good deed.
2 TIMOTHY 3:15-17

I have hidden your word in my heart
that I might not sin against you.
PSALM 119:11

The word of God is alive and active. It cuts more keenly than any two-edged sword, piercing so deeply that it divides soul and spirit, joints and marrow; it discriminates among the purposes and thoughts of the heart.

HEBREWS 4:12

The Bible is made up of a library of sixty-six books. It can be a daunting task to set off determined to read through them all. It is probably not the most helpful way to begin at Genesis 1 and read right on to the end of Revelation. An easier way is to use one of the Bible-reading schemes that are on the market. These provide a daily plan of readings, with helpful comments on the verses selected for the day. Many of these schemes do in fact cover the whole Bible over a few years. There are also helpful books that explain the background to the Bible, its cultures and its various authors in order to smooth out some of the difficulties we encounter.

It is good sometimes to read a whole book of the Bible at a sitting – preferably in a modern translation – in order to grasp its breadth and scope. And it is specially important to read and re-read the Gospels, so that we can take in more and more about Jesus' life and teaching. John's Gospel calls Jesus the 'Word'. He is God's message to us in the flesh – God's perfect means of communication. As we read about him, we can discover what God is really like.

As we drive or walk or wash the dishes, we can chew over some of the phrases and sentences from the Bible that have helped us. We can learn by heart passages that are specially important in daily living.

There is no substitute for getting to know and understand the Bible if we are to grow and mature as Christians. It can be described as spiritual food, which nourishes us and helps us to grow spiritually. To use the light metaphor – it shows up the dangers and warns us when we are going the wrong way. It guides us and sheds light on our whole journey to God.

TRAVELLERS' TALES

Martin Luther went to great lengths, as a monk, to find salvation and a right relationship with God. But he was still plagued by guilt. Then, one day, when he was reading Paul's letter to the Romans, light dawned. He realized that God forgives on the basis of faith alone – and his life was transformed. One of his great achievements was to translate the Bible into German, so that ordinary people could read it.

Oh! how great and glorious a thing it is to have before one the Word of God! With that we may at all times feel joyous and secure; we need never be in want of consolation, for we see before us, in all its brightness, the pure and right way. He who loses sight of the Word of God, falls into despair; the voice of heaven no longer sustains him; he follows only the disorderly tendency of his heart, and of world vanity, which lead him on to his destruction.

FROM *TABLE TALK*, MARTIN LUTHER (1483-1546)

It is the task of the Word of God to be our guardian, our moral and spiritual instructor. He teaches us to love freedom, to love our fellow man, to love and admire what is excellent, rather than merely what is effective or adequate. The Word will not permit us to get away with carelessness or mediocrity.

We all accept that there is special training for philosophers, for teachers, for athletes. Equally, for those who have chosen to major in holiness, there is a special training in the Word... This training (unlike some of the others) does not put people under emotional or physical strain and tension. It is not a matter of driving oneself to the limit so much as allowing the Word to show us our weaknesses and moral flaws, and then bringing us our Saviour's own remedies, precisely gauged to meet every specific need.

CLEMENT OF ALEXANDRIA (155-220 AD)

It is for truth, not for literary excellence, that we go to
Holy Scripture... Mankind is always changing; God's truth
stands for ever... You will get most out of it if you read it
with humility, and simplicity, and faith.

FROM *IMITATION OF CHRIST*, THOMAS À KEMPIS (1380-1471)

J.B. Phillips recorded his experience as a Bible translator:

The New Testament, given a fair hearing, does not need
me or anyone else to defend it. It has the proper ring for
anyone who has not lost his ear for truth... As the years
have passed... my conviction has grown that the New
Testament is in a quite special sense inspired. It is not
magical, nor is it faultless: human beings wrote it. But by
something which I would not hesitate to describe as a
miracle, there is a concentration upon that area of inner
truth which is fundamental and ageless. That, I believe, is
why millions of people have heard the voice of God
speaking to them through these seemingly artless pages.

FROM *RING OF TRUTH*, J.B. PHILLIPS

Lord, here is my Bible,
Here is this quiet room, here is this quiet time, and here am I.
Open my eyes; open my heart; and speak.

DICK WILLIAMS, FROM *PRAYERS FOR TODAY'S CHURCH*

Eternal God, all-powerful and merciful,
your word is a torch for our path
and a light for our way.
Open our eyes and enlighten our spirit
that we may understand your revelation
in all its purity and holiness.
May it transform our lives
and make us worthy to bear your image;
through Jesus Christ our Lord. Amen.

ULRICH ZWINGLI (1484-1531), SWISS REFORMER. FROM *A BOOK OF VESTRY PRAYERS*

For Reflection

God's Word, the Bible, spotlights God's living Word, Jesus.

A World to Care for

GOD'S CREATION

When I was about three years old, the next-door neighbour's dog died. I don't know who broke the news to me but I well remember standing our side of the dividing fence while 'The-Lady-At-Number-One' stood her side. The difference in our ages did not seem to matter. We cried together in shared grief as we mourned the dog we had both loved and whose faithful companionship had meant so much in our lives.

God created men and women with a mandate to look after his world. They were to harness its resources well and to order and care for the animal creation. But men and women chose to go their own way instead of obeying God's wise directions and as a result the delicate balance of nature has been disturbed. The earth is subject to natural disasters; men and women have ruthlessly raped the earth's resources. Deserts and dustbowls replace fertile land and forests teeming with life. The earth is scarred and the sea and near space littered with our rubbish.

We have misused the animal kingdom too. Species have been hunted to extinction and domestic animals have been ill-treated, sometimes the objects of gratuitous cruelty and inhumane factory-farming.

We still enjoy the beauty of the world and the loyalty and affection of domestic animals. But as members of the human race we need to repent. Care of the earth and care for animals was our responsibility as God's stewards, and we have failed.

Bible Signposts

So God created human beings, making them to be like
himself. He created them male and female, blessed them,
and said, 'Have many children, so that your descendants
will live all over the earth and bring it under control. I am
putting you in charge of the fish, the birds, and all the wild
animals.'

GENESIS 1:26-28

Jesus said: 'Look at the birds flying around: they do not
sow seeds, gather a harvest and put it into barns; yet your
Father in heaven takes care of them! Aren't you worth
much more than birds?... Look how the wild flowers grow:
they do not work or make clothes for themselves... It is
God who clothes the wild grass... Won't he be all the more
sure to clothe you?'

MATTHEW 6:26-30

The whole creation is on tiptoe to see the wonderful sight
of the children of God coming into their own. The world
of creation cannot as yet see reality, not because it chooses
to be blind, but because in God's purpose it has been so
limited – yet it has been given hope. And the hope is that
in the end the whole of created life will be rescued from the
tyranny of change and decay, and have its share in that
magnificent liberty which can only belong to the children
of God!

ROMANS 8:19-21

Relying on God's promise we look forward to new heavens
and a new earth, in which justice will be established.

2 PETER 3:13

The Lord has told us what is good. What he requires of us
is this: to do what is just, to show constant love, and to
live in humble fellowship with our God.

MICAH 6:8

*What good is it, my friends, for someone to say he has
faith when his actions do nothing to show it?... Suppose a
fellow-Christian, whether man or woman, is in rags
without enough food for the day, and one of you says,
'Good-bye, keep warm, and have a good meal,' but does
nothing to supply their bodily needs, what good is that?*
JAMES 2:14-16

*Next a word to you who are rich... You have piled up
wealth in an age that is near its close. The wages you
never paid to the men who mowed your fields are crying
aloud against you, and the outcry of the reapers has
reached the ears of the Lord of Hosts. You have lived on
the land in wanton luxury.*
JAMES 5:1, 4, 5

Men and women are not merely the highest form of animal life.
We alone of God's creation have been made in God's image
and because of that we are of value in a unique way. All
creation reflects God's glory but we alone were created to be in
loving and obedient relationship with him. God's image has
been sadly defaced in all of us, but God's plan is to restore it
when we receive new life through Jesus. Our broken
relationship with God is mended and the Holy Spirit is at work
to heal our relationships with one another too. God intended
us to live together in harmony, showing justice, compassion
and mutual respect, irrespective of sex, race, colour, intellect or
social status.

From the beginning human relationships have been spoiled
by jealousy, cruelty, exploitation and selfishness. And clearly we
are not learning from past mistakes or evolving into a better
society. Our century has witnessed more inhumanity, war,
suffering and persecution than any before.

There seems to be so little that any of us can do to care for
our world and to show God's love and justice to those who live
in it. How are we to respond to the enormous human need and

to the constant demands on our compassion – and our purses – in the global village which our world has become? How can we share God's love in practical ways among the people who are our neighbours – whether they live in our town or in a country we have never visited?

In the past, individual Christian men and women have spearheaded many just causes – the rights of slaves, of child labourers, of black people... Many today have organized life-giving aid programmes, communicating the good news of Jesus in varied ways. We may feel that we can't achieve much, as individuals, or even as part of a local church, and we certainly cannot touch every area of need. But we can take time and trouble to find out what other Christians are doing in our world, ready to respond as God brings home to us specific needs. Then we can 'light a candle' by our concern, our prayers, and by giving our money, time and skills for the healing of God's world. We can pray, too, for the coming of that day of restoration when God, through Jesus, will make all things new.

TRAVELLERS' TALES

The world is charged with the grandeur of God.
It will flame out, like shining from shook foil;
It gathers to a greatness, like the ooze of oil
Crushed. Why do men then now not reck his rod?
Generations have trod, have trod, have trod;
And all is seared with trade; bleared, smeared with toil;
And wears man's smudge, and shares man's smell: the
soil
Is bare now, nor can foot feel, being shod.

And for all this, nature is never spent;
There lives the dearest freshness deep down things;
And though the last lights off the black West went

Oh, morning, at the brown brink eastward, springs –
Because the Holy Ghost over the bent
World broods with warm breast and with ah! bright
wings.

GERARD MANLEY HOPKINS (1844-89)

In the morning when the sun rises, everyone ought to
praise God who created it for our use, because thanks to
it our eyes are enlightened by day. Then in the evening,
when it gets dark, everyone ought to give praise on
account of Brother Fire, thanks to whom our eyes are
enlightened by night. And therefore we ought especially to
praise the Creator himself for this and the other creatures
which we daily use.

FROM *MIRROR OF PERFECTION* CXIX, FRANCIS OF ASSISI (1182-1226)

Enjoy the earth gently
Enjoy the earth gently
For if the earth is spoiled
It cannot be repaired
Enjoy the earth gently.

YORUBA POEM, WEST AFRICA

In 1980 Oscar Romero, archbishop of San Salvador, was shot
as he celebrated mass at the altar of his cathedral. He had
antagonized both right and left wing parties because he bravely
championed the cause of the poor and upheld justice:

If we illuminate with Christian hope those longings for
justice, peace and goodness that we still have on this earth,
they will be realized... Such has been the reward of all of
those who do that work, watering the earth with truth,
love and kindness. These deeds are not lost; purified by the
spirit of God, their effects are our reward.

FROM *PRAYERS FOR PEACE*, RUNCIE AND HUME

*When you look at someone with eyes of love, you see a
reality different from that of someone who looks at the
same person without love, with hatred or even just with
indifference.*

ARCHBISHOP DESMOND TUTU, HOPE AND SUFFERING

*Be kind and merciful. Let no one ever come to you
without coming away better and happier. Be the living
expression of God's kindness: kindness in your face,
kindness in your eyes, kindness in your smile, kindness
in your warm greeting. In the slums we are the light of
God's kindness to the poor. To children, to the poor, to
all who suffer and are lonely, give always a happy smile
– Give them not only your care, but also your heart.*

MOTHER TERESA OF CALCUTTA

This poem was written by Ernesto Castillo, a Nicaraguan
revolutionary fighter, killed on 9 September 1978, aged 20.

*Where the unknown
have shed their blood,
where they have left
a dust-smelling
memory,
that's where I'll start
building hope and joy.
Where the guards
set fire to farms,
where the aeroplane bombed
villages,
we will put up schools,
co-operatives,
hospitals,
called by the names of those
who died without seeing them.*

FROM POETS OF THE NICARAGUAN REVOLUTION

To you, Creator of nature and humanity, of truth and
beauty, I pray:

Hear my voice, for it is the voice of the victims of all
wars and violence among individuals and nations.

Hear my voice, for it is the voice of all children who
suffer and will suffer when people put their faith in
weapons and war.

Hear my voice when I beg you to instil into the
hearts of all human beings the wisdom of peace, the
strength of justice and the joy of fellowship.

Hear my voice, for I speak for the multitudes in
every country and in every period of history who do not
want war and are ready to walk the road of peace.

Hear my voice and grant insight and strength so that
we may always respond to hatred with love, to injustice
with total dedication to justice, to need with the sharing of
self, to war with peace.

O God, hear my voice, and grant unto the world
your everlasting peace.

POPE JOHN PAUL II

You asked for my hands
that you might use them for your purpose.
I gave them for a moment then withdrew them
for the work was hard.

You asked for my mouth
to speak out against injustice.
I gave you a whisper that I might not be accused.

You asked for my eyes
to see the pain of poverty.
I closed them for I did not want to see.

You asked for my life
that you might work through me.
I gave a small part that I might not get too involved.

Lord, forgive my calculated efforts to serve you,
only when it is convenient for me to do so,
only in those places where it is safe to do so,
and only with those who make it easy to do so.

Father, forgive me,
renew me
send me out as a usable instrument
that I might take seriously
the meaning of your cross.

JOE SEREMANE, SOUTH AFRICA, FROM *LIFELINES*

FOR REFLECTION

Only God can establish justice and peace in our world. But we must begin to help him here and now.

In a Strange Land

THE WORLD WE LIVE IN

*Even though I was very young, I used to be allowed to
stay up for the Sunday evening open-air meetings. Below us
the sea sparkled enticingly. An elderly gentleman with a
snow-white beard reverently turned the pages of an enormous
oil-cloth hymn sheet slung over an easel, so that we could all
see the words to sing. (I thought then that he looked exactly
like God.) One speaker after another, with uplifted voice,
proclaimed the gospel message. And I, in my Sunday best, sat
quietly watching.*

*All around I could see what was clearly 'the world'. I
knew that was so, because these people were doing all the
things that were forbidden to me, or beyond our means.*

*Small children, dressed in bathing suits, who had actually
been allowed to paddle and play on the sands on a Sunday,
now toiled wearily up the zig-zag path from the beach,
clinging to their mothers' hands.*

*Then, from the nearby hotel, guests emerged in long
evening dresses, languid, beautiful and utterly oblivious of our
humble activities, nonchalantly refusing the proffered tracts.*

*I felt confused. I was the inhabitant of two different
worlds.*

'Worldliness' is not heard or preached about now as it once
was. The concept comes from Jesus' own teaching. He told his
disciples that he was going to send them into the world, but
that they did not belong to the world. He warned them that
the world would hate them because they were strangers in the
world just as he had been.

The Bible uses the word 'world' in several different senses. It is used to mean our planet, which God created perfect but which has been spoiled and exploited.

The world can also mean the men and women who make up its population. It is used in this sense in the verse 'God so loved the world that he gave his only Son, that everyone who has faith in him may not perish but have eternal life'.

But the world, in its bad sense, means society at loggerheads with God and his people; society organized without reference to God or his laws and completely at variance with Christian values. The lifestyle of the world is geared to achieving personal power or prestige, money, pleasure and glamour. It has no spiritual dimension and takes no account of life beyond death.

Christians down the ages have wrestled with the problem of how to be 'in the world but not of it'. Some early devout ascetics fled to the desert or to solitary caves to avoid the world's contamination. Puritans vetoed all kinds of pleasures, including even mincepies and the celebration of Christmas. A generation or two ago many religious people interpreted worldliness to mean the use of make-up or going to theatres and cinemas. Mixing with 'the world' was wrong – Christians, wherever possible, should keep to the company of other Christians only.

We no longer interpret Jesus' words about the world in such limited and simplistic ways. We recognize our responsibility to live in the world, spreading salt and light – as Jesus put it – by living out our Christian faith in family, school or workplace.

But we make a mistake if we imagine that 'worldliness' is dead and gone. In Bible terms, it is still the church's fierce enemy. It is only too easy to take on board the standards of the society we live in. If we are geared to consumerism, aim to satisfy our own needs and desires, or to boost our own egos; if we lay our plans in terms of this life only, then we are living in direct opposition to Jesus' teaching and the manifesto of his kingdom.

Bible Signposts

*Do not set your hearts on the world or what is in it.
Anyone who loves the world does not love the Father.
Everything in the world, all that panders to the appetites
or entices the eyes, all the arrogance based on wealth,
these spring not from the Father but from the world. That
world with all its allurements is passing away, but those
who do God's will remain for ever.*

1 JOHN 2:15-17

*Pure and faultless religion in the sight of God the Father is
this: to look after orphans and widows in trouble and to
keep oneself untarnished by the world.*

JAMES 1:27

*Jesus said in his prayer for his followers: 'The world hates
them because they are strangers in the world, as I am. I do
not pray you to take them out of the world, but to keep
them from the evil one'.*

JOHN 17:14-15

*Jesus told his followers: 'You are salt to the world...You are
light for all the world.'*

MATTHEW 5:13-14

*Don't let the world around squeeze you into its own
mould, but let God remould your minds from within.*

ROMANS 12:2

*We... are citizens of heaven, and from heaven we expect
our deliverer to come, the Lord Jesus Christ.*

PHILIPPIANS 3:20

*The 'heroes of faith' , described in the New Testament
letter to the Hebrews: 'admitted openly that they were
foreigners and refugees on earth... It was a better country
they longed for, the heavenly country'.*

HEBREWS 11:13-16

Christian faith is not negative. We don't have to 'give up' the world – instead we receive citizenship of a far better country. Paul, writing to Christians at Philippi, describes the Christians as citizens of heaven – those who abide by the standards and enjoy the benefits of God's kingdom. Philippi was a colony of Rome. As such, Philippians had all the advantages and privileges reserved for Roman citizens. They wore the toga and were proud to be a little bit of Rome set down in the middle of another culture.

We take pride in our 'citizenship' too. We own Jesus as king and follow his laws. We enjoy the benefits and privileges of belonging to his kingdom. Our ultimate goal is the Homeland itself.

TRAVELLERS' TALES

What should we do about those around us who are not believers? Certainly we should pray for them, not just occasionally or as a matter of routine but all the time, in the hope that they may have a change of heart and so find their way to God.

But we should also give them every opportunity to learn the truth of Christ from us, not so much, perhaps, by our preaching it to them in so many words, but by the way we behave towards them. Our attitude should reflect the attitude of Christ...

At the same time, don't compromise your beliefs or water them down to make them acceptable. It is possible to stand firm against violence and error while remaining perfectly calm and gentle. Don't be trapped into playing their game with them!... Our attitude should be that of the Lord Jesus. If we imitate him, we won't go wrong.

IGNATIUS OF ANTIOCH (C.35-C.107 AD)

I don't believe that the economic and erotic motive account for everything that goes on in what we moralists call the World. Even if you add Ambition I think the picture is still incomplete...We hope, no doubt, for tangible profits from every Inner Ring we penetrate: power, money, liberty to break rules, avoidance of routine duties, evasion of discipline. But all these would not satisfy us if we did not get in addition the delicious sense of secret intimacy... This desire is one of the factors which go to make up the world as we know it – this whole pell-mell of struggle, competition, confusion, graft, disappointment and advertisement... Unless you take measures to prevent it, this desire is going to be one of the chief motives of your life... If you do nothing about it, if you drift with the stream, you will in fact be an 'inner ringer'...The quest of the Inner Ring will break your hearts unless you break it.

FROM *TRANSPOSITION AND OTHER ADDRESSES*, C.S. LEWIS

We let the world overcome us; we live too much in continual fear of the chances and changes of mortal life. We let things go too much their own way. We try too much to get what we can by our own selfish wits, without considering our neighbours. We follow too much the ways and fashions of the day, doing and saying and thinking anything that comes uppermost, just because there is so much around us. Free us from our selfish interests, and guide us, good Lord, to see your way, and to do your will.

CHARLES KINGSLEY (1819-75)

I am come from the City of Destruction, and am going to Mount Sion.

CHRISTIAN, FROM *PILGRIM'S PROGRESS*, JOHN BUNYAN

God, our promised land;
Christ, our way,
our journey has become long and hard
because we wander about
like nomads

not knowing where to go.
We are strangers in our own land,
without bread, a roof, a future.
But you came to find us
with your life-giving breath.
You, who are also displaced,
have become an exile with us.
You offer us anew the promised land.
Your spirit urges us toward
that joyous homecoming.
DISPLACED CAMPESINOS, LIMA, PERU

You can't tell a Christian from a non-Christian by where
he lives, or the way he speaks or how he dresses. There are
no 'Christian towns', there is no 'Christian language', and
they eat, drink and sleep just like everybody else.
Christians aren't particularly clever or ingenious, and they
haven't mastered some complicated formula, like the
followers of some religions. But while it's true that they live
in cities next to other people, and follow the same pattern
of life as they do, in fact they have a unique citizenship of
their own. They are, of course, citizens of their own lands
– loyal ones, too. But yet they feel like visitors. Every
foreign country is their homeland, and their homeland is
like a foreign country to them.
EPISTLE TO DIOGNETUS C.150 AD

For Reflection

A Christian is in the world but does not belong to it.

Travelling Light

POSSESSIONS

On those seaside holidays long ago, a generous
aunt would rent a beach-hut for us to use. This
miniature house was a child's delight. But furnishings
were few; we only took the bare essentials to the hut.
We used oddments of cutlery and crockery and an old
kettle and brought the provisions we needed each day.

One summer my sister and I were fascinated by
the family in the beach-hut next door. People kept
asking to photograph the father, and eventually we
discovered that he was a famous xylophone player
called Teddy Brown. What amazed us most was the
sumptuousness of their beach hut. It was a hut just
like ours, but they had transformed it. They sat round
a gilded table on gilt chairs and ate royally.
Everything breathed luxury and high living. Even this
temporary 'house' was magnificently furnished, with
no expense spared.

Too many possessions are a hindrance on the journey of
the spirit just as too much baggage can be on any other
journey.

The New Testament often reminds us that our present
life is a very temporary affair. It is a short journey from
birth to death. We need only bivouac – put up a tent –
providing ourselves with the bare essentials. God has a
permanent, solid house ready for us at journey's end.

BIBLE SIGNPOSTS

*Let us strip off everything that hinders us,... and let us run
the race that we have to run with patience, our eyes fixed
on Jesus the source and goal of our faith.*
HEBREWS 12:1-2

*Jesus said: 'Do not store up for yourselves treasure on
earth, where moth and rust destroy, and thieves break in
and steal; but store up treasure in heaven, where neither
moth nor rust will destroy, nor thieves break in and steal.
For where your treasure is, there will your heart be also.'*
MATTHEW 6:19-21

*What did we bring into the world? Nothing! What can we
take out of the world? Nothing! So then, if we have food
and clothes, that should be enough for us. But those who
want to get rich fall into temptation and are caught in the
trap of many foolish and harmful desires, which pull them
down to ruin and destruction. For the love of money is a
source of all kinds of evil. Some have been so eager to have
it that they have wandered away from the faith and have
broken their hearts with many sorrows...*

*Command those who are rich in the things of this life
not to be proud, but to place their hope, not in such an
uncertain thing as riches, but in God, who generously gives
us everything for our enjoyment. Command them to do
good, to be rich in good works, to share with others. In this
way they will store up for themselves a treasure which will
be a solid foundation for the future.*
1 TIMOTHY 6:7-10, 17-19

*A man in the crowd said to Jesus, 'Teacher, tell my brother
to divide with me the property our father left us.'*

*Jesus said, 'Watch out and guard yourselves from
every kind of greed; because a person's true life is not made
up of the things he owns, no matter how rich he may be.'*

Jesus told this parable: 'There was once a rich man who had land which bore good crops. He began to think to himself, "I haven't anywhere to keep all my crops. What can I do? This is what I will do," he told himself; "I will tear down my barns and build bigger ones, where I will store my corn and all my other goods. Then I will say to myself, Lucky man! You have all the good things you need for many years. Take life easy, eat, drink, and enjoy yourself!" But God said to him, "You fool! This very night you will have to give up your life; then who will get all these things you have kept for yourself?"'

And Jesus concluded, 'This is how it is with those who pile up riches for themselves but are not rich in God's sight.'

LUKE 12:13-21

Many of us live in a society where only money talks. Most things – and people – are valued according to their market price. Many people seem to believe that winning a few million on the state lottery or the football pools would be the answer to life's problems.

The Bible takes a different view. It sees nothing wrong in money itself – in fact there are plenty of ways in which it can be used well. But it recognizes that the love of money leads to all kinds of evil. It also points out that money and possessions can actually be a hindrance to right living. They can become so important that they take the place of God in our thoughts and affections. We may find it easier to rely on what we have in the bank than on God's promises.

Christians need to calculate how to 'travel light', using money and possessions to serve God. That is what Jesus called storing up our treasure in heaven. As members of God's family we shall also want to share what we have with others all over the world, who may be without the food, water, clothes, medicines, education or Bibles needed to survive. In giving like this we become 'rich towards God'.

It is not easy knowing how to allocate our money. How much should we spend on ourselves and how much should we give to God? There are no hard and fast rules, though some (like the people of Israel in the Old Testament) give one tenth of their income to Christian work as a minimum contribution. Every one of us must respond as God prompts us. Our lifestyle is not based on rules but on love for God and our neighbour.

TRAVELLERS' TALES

James Hudson Taylor (1832-1905), in many ways an eccentric and extreme in his way of life, had strong views on his need to travel light. He became a pioneer missionary in China and founded the China Inland Mission. He lived and dressed as the local people did and depended entirely on God to supply his needs.

At twenty, he was medical assistant to a doctor in Hull and wrote about his very frugal style of living even then:

I soon found that I could live upon very much less than I had previously thought possible. Butter, milk and other luxuries I ceased to use, and found that by living mainly on oatmeal and rice, with occasional variations, a very small sum was sufficient for my needs. In this way I had more than two-thirds of my income available for other purposes, and my experience was that the less I spent on myself and the more I gave to others, the fuller of happiness and blessing did my soul become.

FROM DR AND MRS HOWARD TAYLOR

Don't despise possessions. And don't despise profits, either. After all, possessions are 'possessed' by us: they are our servants, not our masters. And profits are 'profitable', or they should be.

Wealth is at our disposal, an instrument which can be used well or foolishly. How it is used doesn't depend on the instrument, but on the person who is using it. If we use it well, it is a valuable servant – a servant which can do good things for us, and for those who depend on us. If we use it badly, it is an unhelpful servant – a servant which causes us and our friends endless harm. We shouldn't blame what is harmless. Wealth in itself is neither good nor evil.

So where does the blame lie for all the evil done in the name of money and possessions? Not in the things themselves: they are harmlessly neutral. The evil is in the mind of man himself – man who by the free will and moral independence God has given him manages what he owns. Human desires express themselves through a man's possessions – desire to impress others, perhaps, or competitive instincts, which drive him always to rival his affluent neighbour. But those desires can also be noble ones, and express themselves in noble ways. Our money can feed the hungry and clothe the poor.

CLEMENT OF ALEXANDRIA (155-220 AD)

Our economic laws and principles are a reflection of our values, and our values come from our hearts. 'For where your treasure is, there will your heart be also.' If our treasure is in the balance of payments, then our hearts will be there also: all things and all people will finally be controlled by their price. Market forces will rule.

FROM OH GOD, WHY?, GERARD HUGHES

What are my treasures – the things I value most?
How do they fare when it comes to the last journey of all?
In a word – do they really belong to this world: so that
they stay in it when I leave it?
Or do they belong to the world to come – though
some have their beginnings now?

Mostly, I guess, mine belong here.
So I pray today, while there is still time, that you will wean
me from holding earthly treasures, however good, as closest
to my heart.

Increase my appetite for heavenly treasure
  the knowledge of God
  the friendship of Jesus
  the life of the Spirit,
so that the ties that hold my heart to this present world
begin to loosen –
for where my treasure is, there is my heart also.
And what I ask for myself, help me to seek also for my
friends,
for your Name's sake. Amen.

FROM *SOMEONE WHO BECKONS*, BISHOP TIMOTHY DUDLEY-SMITH

O Lord our God,
give us by your Holy Spirit
a willing heart and a ready hand
to use all your gifts to your praise and glory;
through Jesus Christ our Lord.

THOMAS CRANMER (1489-1556)

FOR REFLECTION

Jesus said: 'You cannot serve God and money'.

Following the Leader

OBEDIENCE

My mother was very anxious that my sister and I should not be too noisy or boisterous for our elderly grandparents. So every day, whatever the weather, she would take us for a walk along the sea cliffs, to get rid of our high spirits. I have vivid memories of the winter seas, crashing over the lower road as we walked along the cliff path above, with its sandy soil and tussocks of coarse grass where delicate tamarisks bloomed in summer.

Our favourite game was 'Follow my leader'. My mother would go ahead and we had to follow exactly in her steps, walking, running, jumping; going round rocks or over them, down into little dells and over sandy humps. It seemed as if the wind was always blowing and the fine rain sleeting in our faces. But we loved the wild freedom of those cliff walks, made all the more exciting by the rules and discipline of our game.

Human beings were created to follow and obey God. But the Bible describes the first sin committed by man and woman as one of disobedience to God. The Evil One encouraged them to doubt the validity and wisdom of going God's way. Their own pride, curiosity and ambition also drove them to take and eat the forbidden fruit. But as soon as they left the path of obedience to God and struck out on their own they hit the trail that leads to death and destruction.

Ever since, men and women have faced the choice of going their own way – listening to the voice of the Evil One, following their own wishes – or obeying God. Temptation always lies in facing this decisive choice – God or me; good or evil.

Jesus is the only person who has ever lived as human beings were intended to live. He resisted all attempts to be drawn away from doing what God wanted. He followed exactly in God's footsteps, even though, for him, it involved suffering and death. In Jesus, we see what human life is meant to be.

BIBLE SIGNPOSTS

Jesus said: 'My food is to obey the will of the one who sent me and to finish the work he gave me to do.'
JOHN 4:34

In the Garden of Gethsemane Jesus prayed: 'Father, my Father! All things are possible for you. Take this cup of suffering away from me. Yet not what I want, but what you want.'
MARK 14:36

Even though he was God's Son, Jesus learnt through his sufferings to be obedient.
HEBREWS 5:8

Bearing the human likeness, sharing the human lot, Jesus humbled himself, and was obedient, even to the point of death, death on a cross!... So you too, my friends, must be obedient, as always.
PHILIPPIANS 2:7-8,12

No one when tempted should say, 'I am being tempted by God'; for God cannot be tempted by evil and does not himself tempt anyone. Temptation comes when anyone is lured and dragged away by his own desires; then desire conceives and gives birth to sin, and sin when it is full-grown breeds death.
JAMES 1:13-15

Be on the alert! Wake up! Your enemy the devil, like a roaring lion, prowls around, looking for someone to devour. Stand up to him, firm in your faith, and remember that your fellow-Christians in this world are going through the same kinds of suffering.

1 PETER 5:8-9

Be obedient to God your Father, and do not let your characters be shaped any longer by the desires you cherished in your days of ignorance.

1 PETER 1:14

If you think that you are standing firm, take care, or you may fall. So far you have faced no trial beyond human endurance; God keeps faith and will not let you be tested beyond your powers, but when the test comes he will at the same time provide a way out and so enable you to endure.

1 CORINTHIANS 10:12-13

God's will for us is that we should grow like Jesus, choosing more and more to follow our leader in the way we live. Satan, the enemy of God and all goodness, works with our selfish nature to try to pull us away from loving dependence on God. To do what God wants is not to be controlled by an authoritarian ruler. We were created to live in harmony and loving dependence on God and when we follow his way of love we discover what it means to be truly human.

Many Christians want to follow Jesus' lead but worry about how to discover what God wants them to do when there are specific decisions to be made. Knowing the right path to take does not depend on having a hotline to heaven. It comes as our relationship with our heavenly Father grows and develops. As we keep close to God, we shall gain clearer insights into his plans for us. There are various different ways in which God makes a course of action known. We may experience inner certainty, even a definite 'call'. Circumstances may work together to clarify a decision; doors may open – or close – and we may benefit from the advice of wise Christian friends. No two experiences are ever exactly alike. But God is a loving Father; he will not let any of his children go in the wrong direction, if they truly want to follow his plans. What matters is that we should be honest with ourselves and with God. We must genuinely want to go God's way – not our own.

TRAVELLERS' TALES

There are two ways of living, under two sources of power. One is the way of light, the other the way of darkness. The first way is lit by the angels of God; the second is overshadowed by the angels of Satan.

The way of light is not easy. The pilgrim along this road will find his journey home is a hard and long one. But to help him on his way the Lord has set many lights and many signposts.

The lights are the love of the Creator who made him, the power of the Lord of the earth, the glory of the Redeemer who conquered death.

The signposts are ways to follow: singleness of heart; richness of spirit; the rejection of hypocrisy and separation from those who are walking the way of death.

In short, the way of light is the way of God's commandments. Follow them, respect them, obey them and you will find it a path on which none need stumble, and which finally leads men home.

EPISTLE OF BARNABAS (C.120 AD)

How are we to preserve ourselves against the subtleties and deceits of evil? Of ourselves, we cannot. That is why we have to pray, to submit ourselves to the word of God, allowing it to enlighten our minds and hearts. Then we can begin to distinguish between what is creative and what is destructive within our own hearts, thanking God for what is creative and pursuing it, showing him what is destructive and asking to be delivered from it. There is no evil from which he will not rescue us.

FROM OH GOD, WHY?, GERARD HUGHES

It is only because we are identified with Jesus that we can become like him. By being transformed into his image, we are enabled to model our lives on his. By simply following him, we can perform deeds and live a life which is one with the life of Christ. We are now able to render spontaneous obedience to the word of God...The disciple looks solely at his... Master... and has been called to be the 'imitator of God'.

FROM THE COST OF DISCIPLESHIP, DIETRICH BONHOEFFER

Joy, not grit, is the hallmark of holy obedience. We need to be lighthearted in what we do to avoid taking ourselves too seriously. It is a cheerful revolt against self and pride. Our work is jubilant, carefree, merry. Utter abandonment to God is done freely and with celebration... This is a deep resonant joy that has been tempered by the fires of suffering and sorrow – joy through the cross, joy because of the cross.

FROM FREEDOM OF SIMPLICITY, RICHARD FOSTER

I am afraid of saying 'yes', Lord.
Where will you take me?
I am afraid of drawing the longer straw,
I am afraid of signing my name to an unread agreement,
I am afraid of the 'yes' that entails other 'yeses.'
And yet I am not at peace...

O Lord, I am afraid of your demands, but who can resist you?
That your Kingdom may come and not mine,
That your will may be done and not mine,
Help me to say 'yes'.

FROM PRAYERS OF LIFE, MICHEL QUOIST

FOR REFLECTION

In God's will is my peace.
DANTE (1265-1321)

When the Road is Rough

SUFFERING

One day, when I was about three years old, my unmarried aunt was asked to look after me. She had raging toothache at the time and wanted to keep me occupied without too much effort. She decided to make for the beach and was relieved to see that the Punch and Judy man had set up his booth. The performance was in full swing. She hurried across, thankful for some entertainment to distract me. The story had reached the point where Punch, with triumphant squawks, hits Judy, the baby and the policeman with force and gusto. The crowd of children laughed gleefully but I was cut to the heart. I could not bear to see such suffering and cruelty. I burst into tears and sobbed with all my heart – and voice. In vain my aunt tried to pacify me and tell me it was all pretend. I could see that it was not and I refused to be comforted. As my cries grew louder my embarrassed aunt could only pull me away from the crowd and make for home. And all the while I knew nothing about the very real pain of my aunt's toothache.

Many people feel that they cannot believe in a good and loving God when they see the sum total of suffering in our world or come into close contact with one particular victim of tragedy. Christians have no easy solution to offer. We recognize that pain and sorrow are part of our world because, from the very beginning, man and woman refused God's good way and chose their own path, throwing the whole world system out of gear. We also believe that God has given us freewill – or the freedom to choose – and therefore at times to make wrong choices. Bad choices can have disastrous consequences. But we are still left to wrestle with how God can be both all-powerful and wholly loving. Why doesn't God intervene on behalf of so many innocent victims?

We cannot supply all the answers. But there are facts that we can confidently claim. We know for sure that God is neither remote nor uncaring. In Jesus he came to our world and endured the worst that humankind could do to him. He was tortured, betrayed, forsaken, treated with the most extreme cruelty – physical and mental – and finally put to death. He is the God who shares our suffering and suffers with us.

But Christians do not only believe in a God who allowed himself to be a victim. We believe in a God who is victor – over death and every kind of evil. The cross is the symbol of death but it has also become the symbol of victory. One day justice will be established in the world and sufferers will be comforted and vindicated.

BIBLE SIGNPOSTS

The prophet Isaiah described God's servant, who would suffer on behalf of his people. The early church recognized in Jesus the fulfilment of these words:

> Spurned and withdrawing from human society,
> he was a man who suffered;
> pain was his close acquaintance.
> Like one who must hide his face from us
> he was despised;
> we held him of no account.
> And yet –

they were our sufferings that weighed on him;
our pains were the burden he bore.
While we –
We counted him smitten by God,
struck down by God,
humiliated by God!
But he –
he was pierced by our rebellions,
crushed by our misdeeds;
his burden was the suffering that made us whole,
he endured pain that brought healing to us.
While we –
we were the guilty;
we had strayed like sheep,
each going his own way.
But God!
God burdened him
with the punishment for the guilt of us all.
He was oppressed;
he was struck down.
He said nothing.
He was taken away –
like a sheep to slaughter
like a ewe to the shearers.
He said nothing.
He was silent.
He was arrested;
he was sentenced.
He was taken away;
no one raised a protest at his fate.
He was cut off from the land of life,
struck down because of the guilt of his people.
He was assigned a grave with the wicked,
a burial place with criminals –

for he had practised non-violence,
and had never spoken dishonestly!

FROM ISAIAH 53, TRANSLATED BY PROFESSOR D.J.A. CLINES

The Lord who created you says,
'Do not be afraid – I will save you.
I have called you by name – you are mine.
When you pass through deep waters, I will be with
you;
your troubles will not overwhelm you.
When you pass through fire, you will not be burnt;
the hard trials that come will not hurt you.
For I am the Lord your God,
the holy God of Israel, who saves you...
Do not be afraid – I am with you!'

ISAIAH 43:1-5

What can separate us from the love of Christ? Can
trouble do it, or hardship or persecution or hunger or
poverty or danger or death?... No, in all these things
we have complete victory through him who loved us!
For I am certain that nothing can separate us from his
love: neither death nor life, neither angels nor other
heavenly rulers or powers, neither the present nor the
future, neither the world above nor the world below –
there is nothing in all creation that will ever be able to
separate us from the love of God which is ours
through Christ Jesus our Lord.

ROMANS 8:35-39

This small and temporary trouble we suffer will bring
us a tremendous and eternal glory, much greater than
the trouble. For we fix our attention, not on things
that are seen, but on things that are unseen. What can
be seen lasts only for a time, but what cannot be seen
lasts for ever.

2 CORINTHIANS 4:17-18

Christians are not exempt from suffering. They are just as exposed as everyone else to personal pain and loss. Jesus was called 'a man of sorrows and acquainted with grief' not only because of his own suffering but also because he came close to those in pain and shared their troubles. As his followers, we are called to do the same. Christians have always been among the first to bring aid to victims of war, want and disease. Wherever they live and whatever their job, Christians are called not only to endure pain and suffering themselves but to stand alongside friends and neighbours who are going through personal grief. They are to love, pray, and care for those in trouble.

Job – whose story is told in the Old Testament book of that name – never solved the mystery of his own suffering, but he was convinced in the end of God's greatness, his sovereign power and his right to act as he saw best. In the end, our questions too are silenced as we recognize God's greatness, wisdom and love.

We are never asked to go through suffering alone. God promises to be with us in all that we go through. Nothing whatever can separate us from God's love or the companionship of his Spirit.

Being a Christian does not guarantee 'happy endings' in this life. Well-meaning onlookers may quote, 'all things work together for good to those who love God' as if it were a talisman against the worst distresses of life. But we do not always see things working out well. God is not like some divine puppeteer, pulling strings behind the scenes on behalf of his people so that everyone lives happily ever after.

But we do believe in a God who is greater than the forces of evil. We also believe in a God who is constantly creative. He is never out of control – in our world and in our personal lives. God does not send bad things, but if we place our suffering unreservedly in his hands he can make something good come from it. The sufferer is not the only one who will be blessed as a result; love and light can be shed on our dark world from the deepest sorrow, when it is transfigured by God's skilled and loving hands.

TRAVELLERS' TALES

We must persevere in quiet meditation on the life, sayings, deeds, suffering and death of Jesus in order to learn what God promises and what he fulfils. One thing is certain: we must always live close to the presence of God... no earthly power can touch us without his will, and danger can only drive us closer to him. We can claim nothing for ourselves, and yet we may pray for everything. Our joy is hidden in suffering, our life in death....This day of loneliness need not be a lost day, if it helps you to see more clearly the convictions on which you are going to build your life in times to come.

FROM *LETTERS AND PAPERS FROM PRISON*, DIETRICH BONHOEFFER

Fortunately, God does not abandon us; he has come in Jesus Christ to be with us in our struggle throughout our lives. The all-powerful gift of his love is with us always and our suffering, while not a good thing in itself, can help through Jesus Christ to make us even more aware of his saving love.

FROM *PATHWAYS OF PRAYER*, MICHEL QUOIST

Sheila Cassidy first hit the headlines when she was arrested and tortured in Chile because she gave medical help to a revolutionary. She is now Medical Director of a hospice in Plymouth:

I have long since given up asking the 'why' of suffering. It gets me nowhere, and I know when I'm beat. I live quite peaceably in the eye of this theological storm, moving about in the accustomed darkness like a mole in its burrow or a blind woman in the safety of her home. I know less and less, but that which I do know, I know ever more deeply, down in my guts, where true faith lives.

What, then, is the message from this dark, still point, from the eye of the hurricane? I believe it is this: suffering is, in the same way that life is... More important than asking why, we should get in there, be alongside those who suffer. We must plunge in up to our necks in the icy water, the mud and the slurry to hold up the drowning child until he is rescued or dies in our arms.

FROM *GOOD FRIDAY PEOPLE*, SHEILA CASSIDY

Without our suffering, our work would just be social work, very good and helpful, but it would not be the work of Jesus Christ, not part of the Redemption. Jesus wanted to help by sharing our life, our loneliness, our agony, our death. Only by being one with us has he redeemed us. We are allowed to do the same; all the desolation of the poor people, not only their material poverty, but their spiritual destitution, must be redeemed, and we must share it, for only by being one with them can we redeem them, that is, by bringing God into their lives and bringing them to God.

FROM *SOMETHING BEAUTIFUL FOR GOD*, MOTHER TERESA

As I look around it is often the unbeliever who seems to be free and purposeful, confident and assured. In contrast, I often seem to be anxious, unsure, confused, in pain, and sometimes sunk in that dark pit of depression. Although I proclaim that God is real and answers prayer, to be honest he sometimes seems a million miles away and strangely silent to my frightened cries. But I have discovered over the years *that although God never promises to save us from suffering, he does promise to be with us in the midst of it and is himself afflicted by it.*

FROM *FEAR NO EVIL*, DAVID WATSON

I was separated from my loved ones for a long time because of my illness... When I was taken to the hospital, I lay for several months almost completely alone.

But... I was not really alone. One day a sister brought me a crucifix and hung it on the wall opposite my bed. It was a great help to me to gaze at the face of our Lord filled with agony. He who is love, suffered immeasurable pain beneath his crown of thorns, because he loves me. So I was strengthened, and my faith renewed – he is with me! He loves me more than anyone else ever could... A profound peace entered my heart, and I was deeply comforted.

But that was not all. As I gazed at my crucified Lord and absorbed the essence of Jesus, I became able to trust that during my suffering I would become transformed. What we look upon continually, that we shall become... So the misery of my illness was changed into blessing, peace and joy in him.

FROM *THE BLESSINGS OF ILLNESS*, BASILEA SCHLINK

In Susan Howatch's novel *Absolute Truths*, Charles Ashworth, Bishop of Starbridge (who tells the story), is struggling to come to terms with his wife's death. He quotes a favourite Bible verse (Romans 8:28): 'All things work together for good to them that love God.' Dean Aysgarth comments:

'The correct translation of that passage is actually: "All things intermingle for good to them that love God." I know you think I'm a rotten theologian, Charles, but at least my New Testament Greek is sound.'

I flexed my memory to recall the verb under

discussion. 'But what's the point of the alternative translation?'

'It gives you a better impression of synergy – the process where two different things are put together and make something quite new. If you just say: "All things work together for good" – as if the good and bad are stirred together like the ingredients of a cake which later emerges from the oven smelling wonderful – then the man who's dying of cancer will want to punch you on the jaw... because you're implying that his disease is in the end a good thing. But if you say "All things intermingle for good" you're implying that the good and the bad remain quite distinct...The bad really is terrible and the good may seem powerless against that terrible reality, but when the good and the bad intermingle – not merge but intermingle –'

'They form a pattern,' said Jon... 'The darkness doesn't become less dark, but that pattern which the light makes upon it contains the meaning which makes the darkness endurable.'

FROM ABSOLUTE TRUTHS, SUSAN HOWATCH

Even Jesus did not say, 'I have explained the world'. What he did say was, 'I have overcome the world'. And if we can only trust where we cannot see, walking in the light we have, which is often very much like hanging on in the dark; if we do faithfully that which we see to be the will of God in the circumstances evil thrusts upon us, we can rest our minds in the assurance that circumstances which God allows, reacted to in faith and trust and courage, can never defeat purposes which God ultimately wills... Frankly, hard though it be to say so, it is lack of faith not to be able to bear the thought of anything which God allows.

FROM THE WILL OF GOD, LESLIE WEATHERHEAD

128

FOR REFLECTION

God is loving and good. Yet he allows suffering – his own and ours.

Beside Still Waters

TRANQUILITY

When I was eight or nine I used to go to play
with the daughter of an elderly jeweller, whose shop
was in the old High Street of a small town nearby.
The family lived above the shop and their little girl
was allowed to play in a secluded, walled garden,
hidden from the road. No one would have guessed that
garden existed and I never learned who owned it.

I did not much enjoy the games we played but the
garden was pure delight. It was everything that a
secret garden should be; hidden, unfrequented by
grown-ups, safe and beautiful. Fruit trees had been
trained against the high walls, raspberry and
redcurrant bushes were laden and old-fashioned
flowers bloomed freely. There was a lush green lawn.
It was hard to believe that the busy, noisy High Street
was only a few steps away. It was harder still to leave
our paradise and return to the routine reality of
everyday life.

The Christian life is not all hardship and struggle. It is easy to
dwell on the roughness of the road and to forget the smooth
stretches that are also part of the Christian path. Sometimes
we are aware that life is good. God seems real and near; friends
are congenial; the family rewarding; the circumstances of life
are pleasant. We know that such stretches of the journey will
not last for ever, but we thank God and relish them when they
come our way. We believe they can strengthen and refresh us
for what may lie ahead.

BIBLE SIGNPOSTS

Every good and perfect gift is from above, coming down from the Father.

JAMES 1:17

God... generously gives us everything for our enjoyment.

1 TIMOTHY 6:17

The Lord is my shepherd; I shall not want.
He maketh me to lie down in green pastures,
he leadeth me beside the still waters.
He restoreth my soul.
He leadeth me in the paths of righteousness
for his name's sake.
Yea, though I walk through the valley of the shadow of death,
I will fear no evil, for thou art with me;
thy rod and thy staff they comfort me.
Thou preparest a table before me in the presence of mine enemies,
thou anointest my head with oil;
my cup runneth over.
Surely goodness and mercy shall follow me all the days of my life,
and I will dwell in the house of the Lord for ever.

PSALM 23

I have said to the Lord, 'You are my Lord;
from you alone comes the good I enjoy...
the lines fall for me in pleasant places;
I am well content with my inheritance'.

PSALM 16:2,6

You, Lord, give perfect peace
to those who keep their purpose firm
and put their trust in you.

ISAIAH 26:3

Jesus said: 'Come to me, all who are weary and whose load is heavy; I will give you rest. Take my yoke upon you, and learn from me, for I am gentle and humble-hearted; and you will find rest for your souls. For my yoke is easy to wear, my load is light.'
MATTHEW 11:28

Jesus said: 'Set your troubled hearts at rest. Trust in God always; trust also in me.'
JOHN 14:1

Jesus said: 'In me you may find peace. In the world you will have suffering. But take heart! I have conquered the world.'
JOHN 16:33

You can throw the whole weight of your anxieties upon God, for you are his personal concern.
1 PETER 5:7

There still exists, therefore, a full and complete rest for the people of God... Let us then be eager to know this rest for ourselves, and let us beware that no one misses it through falling into... unbelief.
HEBREWS 4:9,11

Rest and refreshment are not only the outcome of happy circumstances and healthy minds. Many of us know Christians who are coping with difficult situations or chronic pain, yet who carry with them an aura of peace and freedom from tension that is clearly not the product of congenial circumstances.

We have to allow for differences in temperament, but whatever our natural inclinations we need consciously to 'enter into God's rest'. We must bring the peace and security of God's presence and his promises into our busy, stressful lives. Such restfulness of spirit comes from spending time with God and from a conscious move from fear to faith. It takes practice for most of us to replace anxiety with faith in God. It can seem irresponsible to leave go of our worries. Shouldn't we expect to feel burdened? But Jesus taught us to trust our Father implicitly.

We are not responsible for making a success of our Christian lives by our own efforts only. We may offload the responsibility onto God, who is already at work in us by his Spirit. He will give us the help we need as we ask him for it. God does not intend us to be tense or harassed. He wants to give us now a foretaste of the joy and rest we shall know fully and uninterruptedly when our journey is done.

TRAVELLERS' TALES

The peace which comes from the perfect relationship with God... is the goal of the Christian life. It is not the end of activity but the end of all futile striving, in uninterrupted fellowship with God. Through Christ we may begin to share that experience here and now.
FROM *THE EPISTLE TO THE HEBREWS* WILLIAM NEIL DD

We often undervalue the importance of rest in our daily lives because we fail to see the connection between rest and contentment. Without the contentment there can be no true rest. Unless we are content with God and his relationship with us, we will continue searching for answers elsewhere... Our salvation and strength come through rest and trust. With these we will not need to wander aimlessly or search desperately... we can rest confidently in the loving presence of our God.
JANET WELLS

Lord my God,
grant us your peace;
already, indeed, you have made us rich in all things!

Give us that peace of being at rest,
that sabbath peace, the peace which knows no end.

FROM CONFESSIONS, AUGUSTINE OF HIPPO (354-430)

You are giving me, here and now, inward peace and
complete relaxation and a mind turned towards
yourself.

Jesus said, 'Have faith in God.' Therefore it must
be possible, and is made possible by affirmation, and by
acting as though it were possessed already.

Jesus said, 'Fear not.' Therefore it must be
possible, and is made possible by affirmation, by acting
as though one were not afraid.

Jesus said, 'My joy I give unto you.' I accept his
gift. I am going to enjoy today and not let it be spoiled
by apprehension about an unknowable future, by the
demons of fear and worry, by grumbling or self-pity.

Jesus said, 'All things whatsoever you pray and
ask for, believe that you have received them and you
shall have them.'

FROM A PRIVATE HOUSE OF PRAYER, LESLIE WEATHERHEAD

Let us never seek out of thee what we can find only in
thee, O Lord: peace and rest and joy and bliss, which
abide in thee alone.

Lift up our souls above the weary round of
harassing thoughts to thy eternal presence.

Lift up our minds to the pure, bright, serene light
of thy presence, that there we may repose in thy love
and be at rest from ourselves and all things that weary
us; and thence return, arrayed in thy peace, to do and
to bear whatsoever shall best please thee, O blessed
Lord.

E.B. PUSEY (1800-82)

FOR REFLECTION

Complete trust brings perfect peace.

Through the Desert

DISCOURAGEMENT

When I was small I had to have my tonsils removed. My parents booked me into a London nursing home where I had a room on my own. My mother was allowed to visit at any time, but not to stay the night. Every evening she would sit with me until I went to sleep, but the night before I was due to come home I could not sleep. My mother kept stealing towards the door and I kept calling her back. Finally she had to leave to catch the last train home and I was still awake. I shall never forget the sense of loss and of fear when she went and I was left entirely alone.

In a panic I rang the bell for the night nurse. She was less than sympathetic. She told me not to be naughty but to go to sleep. The fear and the desolation I experienced in the hours that followed have never quite left me. But the next day my mother came back.

People of God down the ages have endured periods when God seems to be distant or absent altogether. Sometimes there can be a very ordinary explanation. A recent study has shown – what we might have guessed – that mood swings are normal for both men and women. An 'up' period is followed by a 'down'. Some of us, by temperament or chemistry, are more prone than others to such fluctuations, which also affect our spiritual well-being.

New Christians may expect warm, positive feelings all the time and be tempted to feel that they have lost their way or slipped back if they do not have them. But dryness of spirit may mean that God is taking the opportunity to deepen our faith. If our faith can hold on to him through prayer and praise even when he seems far off, our spiritual life will grow stronger. We must cling to the certainty that God is there, even though he seems to be hidden from us for a short while. The warmth and joy of his felt presence will come again.

BIBLE SIGNPOSTS

As a hind longs for the running streams,
so I long for you, my God.
I thirst for God, the living God;
when shall I come to appear in his presence?
Tears are my food day and night,
while all day long people ask me, 'Where is your God?...
I shall wait for God; I shall yet praise him,
my deliverer, my God.
PSALM 42:1-5

Job said: 'If only I could go back to the old days,
to the time when God was watching over me,
when his lamp shone above my head,
and by its light I walked through the darkness!
If I could be as in the days of my prime,
when God protected my home,
while the Almighty was still there at my side...
But now...
I call out to you, God, but you do not answer,
I stand up to plead, but you keep aloof.'
JOB 29:1-5; 30:20

Jesus came from Nazareth in Galilee and was baptized in
the Jordan by John. As he was coming up out of the water,
he saw the heavens open and the Spirit descend on him,

like a dove. And a voice came from heaven, 'You are my beloved Son; in you I take delight.'

At once the Spirit drove him out into the wilderness, and there he remained for forty days tempted by Satan. He was among the wild beasts; and angels attended to his needs.

MARK 1:9-13

On the cross Jesus cried out: 'My God, my God, why have you forsaken me?'

MARK 15:34

Periods of spiritual dryness are not only the result of mood changes. Physical desolation has played its part in the training of God's servants. Many of them went, literally, into the desert. Abraham, Moses, Elijah, John the Baptist, Jesus himself, and the apostle Paul, spent a period of learning and discipline there. They needed that austere experience to fit them for the very special tasks God was calling them to do.

Others of God's people have chosen the desert experience voluntarily, in order to learn new lessons about God. Surprisingly, perhaps, they have recognized these periods of deprivation as fruitful times of learning from God and maturing in faith and prayer.

TRAVELLERS' TALES

Prayers offered in the state of dryness are those which please [God] best... He wants [Christians] to learn to walk and must therefore take away his hand.

FROM THE SCREWTAPE LETTERS, C.S. LEWIS

So long as we have nothing to say to God, nothing to do with him, save in the sunshine of the mind when we feel him near us, we are poor creatures, willed upon, not willing...

FROM *FIRST SERIES; THE ELOI*, GEORGE MACDONALD (1824-1905)

The most usual entrance to contemplation is through a desert of aridity in which, although you see nothing and feel nothing and apprehend nothing and are conscious only of a certain interior suffering and anxiety, yet you are drawn and held in this darkness and dryness because it is the only place in which you can find any kind of stability and peace. As you progress, you learn to rest in this arid quietude, and the assurance of a comforting and mighty presence at the heart of this experience grows on you more and more, until you gradually realize that it is God revealing himself to you in a light that is painful to your nature and to all its faculties, because it is infinitely above them and because its purity is at war with your own selfishness and darkness and imperfection.

FROM *NEW SEEDS OF CONTEMPLATION*, THOMAS MERTON

God did not say, 'You shall not be tempest-tossed, you shall not be work-weary, you shall not be discomforted.' But he said, 'You shall not be overcome.' God wants us to heed these words so that we shall always be strong in trust, both in sorrow and joy.

JULIAN OF NORWICH (B.1342)

The mystics down the centuries have described the 'dark night of the soul'... those periods when God seems strangely silent and absent in spite of personal need. We wonder what he is doing, why he is withholding his presence from us. We pray to him, but the heavens seem as brass and we feel trapped by the prison of our own dark moods. The greatest test of a Christian's life is to live with the silence of God.

FROM *FEAR NO EVIL*, DAVID WATSON

*Often enough when we approach the altar to pray, our
hearts are dry and lukewarm. But if we persevere, there
comes an unexpected infusion of grace, our breast expands,
as it were, and our interior is filled with an overflowing
love.*

BERNARD OF CLAIRVAUX (1090-1153)

St John of the Cross was born in 1542 and spent his life in the
Carmelite order. He tried, with St Teresa, to reform the Calced
Carmelites but was imprisoned by them. It was probably then,
in 1577-78, that he wrote his poem, 'Dark Night', and the
commentary on part of it. He was the first to use the metaphor
of 'the dark night of the soul', but he sees it as a voluntary,
chosen experience:

*Into the darkness of the night
With heartache kindled into love,
O blessed chance!
I went out unobserved,
My house being wrapped in sleep.*

*In this first verse the soul speaks of the way and method
necessary to attain that life of love with God: by setting
out from itself and all things upon which its affection is set,
and by truly dying to these for the sake of the more
delectable life with God. This process it calls the 'dark
night', by which is understood a cleansing contemplation
causing within the soul a negation of self... God starts to
move them on so that they make progress in their spiritual
lives.*

ST JOHN OF THE CROSS (1542-91)

In *Letters from the Desert* Carlo Carretto drew up a plan of
prayer for Christians in our age:

*As long as we pray only when and how we want to, our
life of prayer is bound to be unreal. It will run in fits and*

starts. *The slightest upset – even a toothache – will be enough to destroy the whole edifice of our prayer-life.*

'*You must strip your prayers,*' *the novice-master told me.*

'*You must simplify, deintellectualize. Put yourself in front of Jesus as a poor man: not with any big ideas, but with living faith. Remain motionless in an act of love before the Father. Don't try to reach God with your understanding; that is impossible. Reach him in love; that is possible.*

FROM *LETTERS FROM THE DESERT*, CARLO CARRETTO

We are never so near God as when we have to get on as well as we can without the consolation of feeling his presence.

FROM *LETTERS OF DIRECTION*, ABBE DE TOURVILLE

FOR REFLECTION

Don't try to reach God with your understanding... Reach him in love.

Travelling Hopefully

HOPE

*When I was five, we prepared for the eventful
journey to London to live with our father again in the
house he had rented. A huge steam train drew up at
the platform, puffing and snorting. My grandfather
came on board with our cases, and I was afraid that he
would be carried off to London too. We gave him a last
goodbye hug and kiss and he climbed down, to wave
from the platform. It was all so strange and I was a
little frightened. But I was also excited at the prospect
of new things to come. Above all, I was serene in the
certainty that my father would meet us at the end of
the journey. I was going to see him again and this time
we would not be parted. I loved and trusted him
utterly, so I made the journey to our new home with
confidence and hope.*

We live in a cynical age, when most people learn quite young
that nothing comes up to expectations. So the word 'hope'
often contains within it elements of despair or the fear of
inevitable disappointment. We are afraid to hope for anything
good, believing that it is better not to hope than to be
disillusioned. If we keep our expectations low we need not feel
let down or suffer the pain of disappointment.

But for the Christian, the word 'hope' has a different ring.
It is not associated with fantasy, day-dreams or an over-
optimistic view of life. Christian hope is securely founded on
the promises of God. And God never breaks his word.

BIBLE SIGNPOSTS

It was by hope that we were saved; but if we see what we hope for, then it is not really hope. For who hopes for something he sees? But if we hope for something we do not see, we wait for it with patience.

ROMANS 8:24-25

We never become discouraged. Even though our physical being is gradually decaying, yet our spiritual being is renewed day after day. And this small and temporary trouble we suffer will bring us a tremendous and eternal glory, much greater than the trouble. For we fix our attention, not on things that are seen, but on things that are unseen. What can be seen lasts only for a time, but what cannot be seen lasts for ever.

2 CORINTHIANS 4:16-18

I wait for the Lord with longing;
I put my hope in his word.
My soul waits for the Lord
more eagerly than watchmen for the morning.
Like those who watch for the morning,
let Israel look for the Lord.
For in the Lord is love unfailing,
and great is his power to deliver.

PSALM 130:1-7

May God, who is the ground of hope, fill you with all joy and peace as you lead the life of faith until, by the power of the Holy Spirit, you overflow with hope.

ROMANS 15:13

'Do not be worried and upset,' Jesus told them. 'Believe in God and believe also in me. There are many rooms in my Father's house, and I am going to prepare a place for you. I would not tell you this if it were not so. And after I go and prepare a place for you, I will come back and take

you to myself, so that you will be where I am.
JOHN 14:1-3

*For God has revealed his grace for the salvation of all
mankind. That grace instructs us to give up ungodly living
and worldly passions, and to live self-controlled, upright
and godly lives in this world, as we wait for the blessed
Day we hope for, when the glory of our great God and
Saviour Jesus Christ will appear.*
TITUS 2:11-13

*Do not, therefore, throw away your confidence, for it
carries a great reward. You need endurance in order to do
God's will and win what he has promised. For, in the
words of scripture, 'very soon he who is to come will come;
he will not delay.'*
HEBREWS 10:35-37

*Here is something, dear friends, which you must not
forget: in the Lord's sight one day is like a thousand years
and a thousand years like one day. It is not that the Lord
is slow in keeping his promise, as some suppose, but that he
is patient with you. It is not his will that any should be
lost, but that all should come to repentance. But the day of
the Lord will come...*
1 PETER 3:8-10

Christian hope is certain. We wait eagerly and expectantly for
God to keep his promises. The Bible is full of what God is ready
to do for his people and we can bank on these promises by
faith. The hope that we have for the future makes looking
ahead positive and encouraging. Many people fear what may lie
ahead: ill-health, unemployment, bereavement and loss, old
age and death itself. Christians can be certain that whatever
happens Jesus will be with them in it. They also know that
however bad things may be, God is able to bring something

positive and good from it. Nothing can separate us from God's love. Whatever life throws at us, the God who loves us is with us in it, bringing his plans to pass.

Jesus has promised us a home 'in his Father's house' when this life is over. The difficulties of the journey will be more than compensated for by the eternal joy of being in God's presence. The road to the Father's country may be hard, especially towards the end of our travels, but the glory that awaits us at journey's end is certain and sure.

There is one special hope for the future, so certain and acknowledged that the Bible often refers to it simply as 'the Day' or 'that Day'. It is the 'Day' when Jesus will come again to this world. The Bible stresses that it will happen, in spite of the long delay. It will be a day of fulfilment and joy for all Jesus' followers, but a day of reckoning for those who have deliberately turned their backs on God. On that day Jesus, who came to earth to be our Saviour, will be God's chosen Judge.

TRAVELLERS' TALES

It is more prudent to be a pessimist. It is an insurance against disappointment, and no one can say 'I told you so,' which is how the prudent condemns the optimist. The essence of optimism is that it takes no account of the present, but it is a source of inspiration, of vitality and hope where others have resigned; it enables a man to hold his head high, to claim the future for himself and not to abandon it to his enemy.

FROM *LETTERS AND PAPERS FROM PRISON*, DIETRICH BONHOEFFER

A man or woman without hope in the future cannot live creatively in the present. The paradox of expectation indeed is that those who believe in tomorrow can better live today, that those who expect joy to come out of sadness can discover the beginnings of a new life in the

centre of the old, that those who look forward to the
returning Lord can discover him already in their midst...

FROM OUT OF SOLITUDE, HENRI NOUWEN

Think of a tree, when you are tempted to feel that God's
promises are delayed, or begin to doubt that the Lord will
come again... Think of a tree, because the process of
growth there is also slow, but inevitable... No stage can be
left out. There are no short cuts to a crop of good, mature
fruit.

Neither can God's purposes be hurried. No stage
can be left out. The whole process must take place. But let
us be in no doubt that his promises will be fulfilled. 'He
will surely come quickly, he will not delay... the Lord, the
Holy One you wait for, will suddenly come to his temple.'
So – be ready!

CLEMENT OF ROME (30-100 AD)

O Lord our God,
fill us with hope
in the shadow of your wings;
protect and sustain us.
You will uphold us,
right from our childhood
until our old age...
It is only close to you
that we find our living goodness,
which is never diminished
since you yourself are goodness...
And if we do not turn aside,
we shall not fail to find
that home, that inheritance
which you have prepared for us.

FROM CONFESSIONS, AUGUSTINE OF HIPPO (354-430)

May the one 'whom we have not seen but yet love'
cause you to rejoice in the hope of seeing him;

May he who is the 'way to the Father'
keep you in an abiding relationship with him;
May he who is going to appear in glory
create in you a motivation to live purely;
May the one who 'will live with his people in the Holy City'
live in peace with you now and forevermore. Amen.
FROM *GENTLE DARKNESS*, ROWLAND CROUCHER

FOR REFLECTION

Hope anchors us safely in the love and promises of God.

Journey's End

LIFE AFTER DEATH

> The aunt who used to rent the beach hut for us was married for five short happy years. She lived with her husband in a flat on the Isle of Wight and we spent one glorious holiday with them. I was delighted with the novelty of being able to lie in bed and watch my aunt getting breakfast in the kitchen opposite.
>
> Before we left to go home her husband, Uncle Walton, gave my sister and me some seeds. I remember now how he bent down to be at our level, showing us the seeds so carefully and explaining how we were to sow them.
>
> 'Next spring,' he told us, 'they will come up and by the summer you will have flowers.' We loved him dearly; he was kind and gentle.
>
> We did not know then why the tears rolled down our mother's face as we eagerly told her about the seeds we were going to plant. She knew – as he knew – that he was terminally ill. When spring came and our seeds grew above ground, he would be dead.

The Bible describes death as 'the last enemy', so it is no wonder that most people are afraid of it – even if they claim to be afraid only of dying, not of what lies beyond. It is a solitary journey into the unknown that all of us must make. Yet for the Christian, death has lost its sting. Whatever our natural, human fear of it we have the sure conviction that Jesus has conquered death, for himself and for all his followers.

Becoming a Christian is sometimes described as receiving 'everlasting' or 'eternal' life, which is the life that belongs to

God, who is eternal. Death has no power to destroy eternal life, which is already pulsing in our veins. When we die we shall enter fully into that life, no longer at the mercy of time or decay. God, our Father, will receive us into his home and into his presence. We shall see him and enjoy that new, abounding life in all its fullness for ever.

BIBLE SIGNPOSTS

Jesus said: 'I am the resurrection. Anyone who believes in me, even though that person dies, will live, and whoever lives and believes in me will never die.'
JOHN 11:25-26

We know that when this tent we live in – our body here on earth – is torn down, God will have a house in heaven for us to live in, a home he himself has made, which will last for ever...
2 CORINTHIANS 5:1

Jesus also became a human being, so that by going through death as a man he might destroy him who had the power of death, that is, the devil; and might also set free those who lived their whole lives a prey to the fear of death.
HEBREWS 2:14-15

Paul wrote to the Christians in Philippi: 'For me life is Christ, and death is gain... I am pulled two ways: my own desire is to depart and be with Christ – that is better by far; but for your sake the greater need is for me to remain in the body.'
PHILIPPIANS 1:21-24

Just as it is our human lot to die once, with judgment to follow, so Christ was offered once to bear the sins of

mankind, and will appear a second time, not to deal with
sin, but to bring salvation to those who eagerly await him.
HEBREWS 9:27-28

Listen, and I will tell you a secret. We shall not all die, but
suddenly, in the twinkling of an eye, everyone of us will be
changed as the trumpet sounds! The trumpet will sound
and the dead shall be raised beyond the reach of
corruption, and we who are still alive shall suddenly be
utterly changed. For this perishable nature of ours must be
wrapped in imperishability, these bodies which are mortal
must be wrapped in immortality. So when the perishable is
lost in the imperishable, the mortal lost in the immortal,
this saying will come true:
  Death is swallowed up in victory.
1 CORINTHIANS 15:51-54

I saw a new heaven and a new earth, for the first heaven
and the first earth had vanished... I heard a loud voice
proclaiming from the throne: 'Now God has his dwelling
with mankind! He will dwell among them and they shall
be his people, and God himself shall be with them. He will
wipe every tear from their eyes. There shall be an end to
death, and to mourning and crying and pain, for the old
order has passed away!'
REVELATION 21:1-4

In past centuries, men and women were ambitious to die a
good death. They wished to be fully prepared to meet their
Maker, to bid a solemn farewell to friends and family and to
speak some well-chosen last words to those gathered around
their death-bed.

Times have changed radically. Not only have most people
today a very different attitude to death and its outcome but
fewer people are conscious or even in their own beds at the

hour of death. Usually the dying person is in hospital, perhaps in intensive care, surrounded by modern equipment and connected to tubes, unaware that these may be his or her last moments. Fewer people deliberately prepare for death – or for the encounter with God to follow.

Whatever our feelings about the painful process of dying, we can look unflinchingly at what lies beyond death. We do not believe in reincarnation. God has made us unique – with one life to live and one death to die. After death God is preparing something for us in his presence that will be unutterably better than anything we have ever known on earth. Our final, resurrection bodies are going to be as superior to our limited, earthly bodies as a solid mansion is to a flimsy tent. Life will be more substantial, more full of enjoyment and fulfilment than anything we have ever experienced on earth. We shall be living the life that God meant his children to live, free from pain, sin, sadness and sorrow.

It is hard to imagine heaven as better and more enjoyable than the best things on earth. But our pleasures will be more real, not less. The book of Revelation uses pictures of food, marriage and music to try to help us understand how fully satisfying heaven will be. At the centre of it all will be Jesus. Our knowledge of him now is dim and faltering, but then we shall experience the total fulfilment of being with him and seeing him face to face.

Our sadness at the death of Christians who are near and dear to us is softened too. We know that they are now in God's presence, free from the limitations of this life.

TRAVELLERS' TALES

During recent years we have come to know death at close quarters. We are surprised ourselves at the placidity with which we hear of the death of one of our contemporaries.

We cannot hate death as we used to, for we have discovered some good in it after all, and have almost come to terms with it. Fundamentally we feel that we really belong to death already, and that every new day is a miracle... We still love life, but I do not think that death can take us by surprise now... It is not the external circumstances, but the spirit in which we face it, that makes death what it can be, a death freely and voluntarily accepted.

DIETRICH BONHOEFFER, *LETTERS AND PAPERS FROM PRISON*

John, called 'Crysostom' – meaning 'golden-mouthed' – was an eloquent speaker and writer. He became bishop of Constantinople, was later banished by the Imperial Court, and died in exile in 407:

Do not give in to grief or despair when someone very dear to you dies. After all, death is a rest, an end to the troubles, anxieties and cares of life. Instead of despairing, stop and think. Reflect that this is the end of every life. Become more kind and thoughtful. Adopt a more reverent attitude towards God. Turn from sin and begin a new and more satisfying style of life.

JOHN CRYSOSTOM (347-407 AD)

Henri Nouwen is a Roman Catholic priest who now works among mentally handicapped people in Canada. Following an accident, when he came close to death, he wrote about his feelings at the time and how the experience changed his life:

No panic, anguish, fear or worry overwhelmed me. I was surprised by my reaction... I knew myself as a very tense, nervous and anxious person. Yet now, in the face of death, I felt only peace, joy and an all-pervading sense of security... I sensed that my life was in real danger. And so I let myself enter into a place I had never been before: the

152

portal of death...What I experienced then was something I had never experienced before: pure and unconditional love. Better still, what I experienced was an intensely personal presence, a presence that pushed all my fears aside and said, 'Come, don't be afraid. I love you.'... He was there, the Lord of my life, saying, 'Come to me, come.'... One emotion was very strong – that of homecoming... The risen Jesus, who now dwells with the Father, was welcoming me home after a long journey...

When I felt my death approaching, I suddenly realized how much I could influence the hearts of those whom I would leave behind... I realized on a very deep level that dying is the most important act of living. It involves a choice to bind others with guilt or to set them free with gratitude... Some people had hurt me deeply, and some had been hurt by me. I experienced a real temptation to hold on to them in anger or guilt. But I also knew that I could choose to let them go and surrender myself completely to the new life in Christ... Dying in Christ can be, indeed, my greatest gift to others.

FROM *BEYOND THE MIRROR*, HENRI NOUWEN

So far as preparing for death goes, I think it is much more a matter of preparing for eternal life. It is a case of getting one's priorities right and living to the full. That is what life is really about, both for oneself and for other people. The actual process of death is just a step in this, like the process of birth... It seems to me that to prepare for death is not suddenly to switch off one's concerns for this world and to start 'thinking of heaven'. It is just trying to live with one's priorities right.

BISHOP JOHN ROBINSON, FROM *DRAWING NEAR TO THE CITY*, SHELAGH BROWN

At least eleven friends gathered around John Wesley's death-bed. One of them, Betsy Ritchie, wrote about his 'good death':

*Finding we could not understand what he said, he paused
a little, and then with all the remaining strength he had,
cried out, 'The best of all is, God is with us'; and then...
lifting up his dying arm in token of victory and raising his
feeble voice with a holy triumph not to be expressed, again
repeated the heart-reviving words, 'The best of all is, God
is with us!'*

FROM *THE JOURNAL OF JOHN WESLEY*

Friar Thomas of Celano, who joined the Franciscan movement
in about 1214, describes the moment of St Francis' death:

*To the doctor who was in attendance, he said: 'Brother
Physician, boldly tell me when death is actually at hand; it
will be the gate to life for me.'*

*With a blithe heart he bade death approach as
though he were talking to a guest:*

'Welcome, my Sister Death!'

FROM *ST FRANCIS AT PRAYER*

I am not dying, I am entering into life.

ST THÉRÈSE OF LISIEUX, ON HER DEATH-BED

*'There was a real railway accident,' said Aslan softly. 'Your
father and mother and all of you are – as you used to call it
in Shadowlands – dead. The term is over: the holidays have
begun. The dream is ended: this is the morning.'...*

*All their life in this world and all their adventures in
Narnia had only been the cover and the title page: now at
last they were beginning Chapter One of the Great Story
which no one on earth has read: which goes on for ever: in
which every chapter is better than the one before.*

FROM *THE LAST BATTLE*, C.S. LEWIS

*Then said Mr Valiant-for-Truth: 'I am going to my fathers,
and though with great difficulty I am got hither, yet now I
do not repent me of all the trouble I have been at to arrive*

where I am... My marks and scars I carry with me, to be a witness for me that I have fought his battles who now will be my rewarder.'

When the day that he must go hence was come many accompanied him to the Riverside, into which, as he went, he said, 'Death, where is thy sting?' And as he went down deeper, he said, 'Grave, where is thy victory?' So he passed over, and the trumpets sounded for him on the other side.

FROM *THE PILGRIM'S PROGRESS*, JOHN BUNYAN

FOR REFLECTION

In our end can be our beginning.

EPILOGUE

Some journeys are a necessary evil. We only decide to set out on them because we particularly want to arrive at our destination. At other times, the journey itself can be part of the pleasure.

When we went on holiday recently, we stopped at a beautiful city on our way and enjoyed looking at lovely buildings and eating good food in pleasant surroundings. When we reached our destination it was the climax to a day of varied pleasures. Of course we also endured the pressure of motorway driving and the frustration of traffic hold-ups, but taking the rough with the smooth, our journey was one to be savoured and remembered with pleasure.

The journey of the spirit, too, has many joys and pleasures along the way. All the good things we enjoy in life come from God. The beauty of the world, the happiness that created things bring to us; the joy of family love and close friendship; the deep rewards of creating for ourselves – music, poetry, food, gardens, beautiful objects – as well as the enjoyment of gifts and skills of others; the satisfying quest for knowledge... The list is endless.

There are also the blessings of the spirit – our response to God and our relationship with him. We enjoy coming close to him in prayer; knowing his nearness in difficulty and trouble; exploring and discovering the treasures of the Bible. We find deep strength and happiness in our oneness with other Christians and in the life of the church. We value many of these experiences all the more as we get further on in our journey. They all help to prepare us for the indescribable joy that we shall know when, the journey done, we come home to God.

Until then – in the words of the Gaelic blessing –

May the road rise to meet you.
May the wind be always at your back.
May the sun shine warm on your face.
May God hold you in the hollow of his hand.

ACKNOWLEDGMENTS

Thanks go to all who have given permission to include material in this book, as indicated in the list below. Every effort has been made to trace and contact copyright owners. We apologise for any inadvertent omissions or errors.

Bible quotations are taken from:
The Good News Bible published by The Bible Societies/HarperCollins*Publishers* Ltd UK © American Bible Society, 1966, 1971, 1976, 1992;
Living Bible copyright © Tyndale House Publishers 1971. All rights reserved;
Holy Bible, New International Version. Copyright © 1973, 1978, 1984 by International Bible Society. All rights reserved;
New Jerusalem Bible © 1985 by Darton, Longman & Todd Ltd and Doubleday and Company, Inc;
J.B. Phillips, © 1960;
Revised English Bible © 1989 by Oxford and Cambridge University Presses.

Michel Quoist: material from *Prayers of Life and Pathways of Prayer* by permission of Gill & Macmillan Publishers (UK); reprinted with permission of Sheed & Ward, 115 E. Armour Blvd., Kansas City, MO 64111 (US).

From *Light through the Curtain*, Lion Publishing, by permission of Keston Institute.

Janet Wells, by kind permission of Scripture Union.

Ernesto Castillo, *Poets of the Nicaraguan Revolution* (translated by Dinah Livingstone, Katabasis 1993).

Susan Howatch from *Absolute Truths*, by permission of
HarperCollins*Publishers* Ltd (UK); Alfred A. Knopf Inc. (US).

Henri Nouwen from *Beyond the Mirror*, HarperCollins*Publishers* Ltd.

Bruce Prewer from *Australian Psalms*. Used by permission of
Openbook Publishers, Adelaide, Australia.

Special thanks to David Winter for his translations from the Early
Church Fathers, taken from *After the Gospels*, Mowbray.

Extract taken from *Letters from the Desert* by Carlo Carretto,
published and copyright 1991 by Darton, Longman and Todd Ltd and
used by permission of the publishers.

Extract taken from *Good Friday People* by Sheila Cassidy, published
and copyright 1991 by Darton, Longman and Todd Ltd and used by
permission of the publishers.